Northwestern University

STUDIES IN *Phenomenology &*

Existential Philosophy

GENERAL EDITOR
John Wild

ASSOCIATE EDITOR
James M. Edie

CONSULTING EDITORS
Herbert Spiegelberg
William Earle
George A. Schrader
Maurice Natanson
Paul Ricoeur
Aron Gurwitsch
Calvin O. Schrag

The Essence of Reasons

Martin Heidegger

Translated by Terrence Malick

The Essence of Reasons

A bilingual edition,
incorporating the German text
of *Vom Wesen des Grundes*

NORTHWESTERN UNIVERSITY PRESS

1 9 6 9 EVANSTON

Contents

Translator's Introduction

HEIDEGGER'S *Vom Wesen des Grundes* first appeared in a *Festschrift* for Edmund Husserl on his seventieth birthday.[1] Following a custom of *Festschrift* contributors, Heidegger used the occasion to settle a number of accounts with his former teacher. During his tenure at the University of Freiburg, Husserl had looked to Heidegger as the inheritor of both his academic chair and his investigations in the theory of knowledge. But with the publication of *Sein und Zeit* in 1927, it became clear that Heidegger was taking an independent stance.[2] Husserl's

1. "Vom Wesen . . . ," in *Ergänzungsband zum Jahrbuch für Philosophie und phänomenologische Forschung* (Halle, 1929), pp. 71–100.
2. Heidegger showed Husserl the rough manuscript of *Sein und Zeit*, his magnum opus, in the spring of 1926, while the two were on vacation at Todtnauberg in the Black Forest. Husserl seems not to have read far into the work; rather he asked Heidegger to edit a student's handwritten

marginalia to the book reveal something more than disappointment. At first he suspects Heidegger of innocently translating his thoughts from "phenomenological" onto "anthropological" terms—writing "Dasein" for Husserl's "ego," *das Man* for "transcendental intersubjectivity," and so forth.[3] Thus many of his following comments deal with Heidegger's misinterpretation of his teachings and consequent lapse into "an intentional psychology of personal-

---

version of his "Vorlesungen zur Phänomenologie des inneren Zeitbewußtseins," a series of lectures which he had delivered at Göttingen in 1904-5. Heidegger agreed to undertake the task once *Sein und Zeit* had been published and his duties at the University of Marburg had terminated, that is, in the fall of 1927. The lectures were published, lightly edited and with a brief introduction, in the 1928 edition of the *Jahrbuch,* Volume IX. Except for the introduction, then, *Vom Wesen des Grundes* was Heidegger's first publication to follow *Sein und Zeit.* As such, it gives, if nothing else, a more trustworthy account of his intentions there than any of his subsequent writings, particularly since 1937, when he feels his thought took a new "turn" (*Kehre*). Cf. his footnote 59, below, p. 96.

3. In his note on page 13, Husserl remarks: "Heidegger transponiert oder transversiert die konstitutiv phänomenologische Klärung aller Regionen des Seienden und Universalen der totalen Region Welt ins Anthropologische. Die ganze Problematik ist Übertragung, dem Ego entspricht Dasein u.s.w., dabei wird alles tiefsinnig unklar und philosophisch verliert es seinen Wert." And on page 62: "Aber wie kann all das anders geklärt werden als durch meine Lehre der Intent. (Geltung) und zunächst der Erfahrenden? Was da gesagt ist ist meine eigene Lehre ohne ihre tiefere Begründung." The marginalia are preserved in the Louvain Archives under the signature "K X Heidegger I." Some have appeared in Alwin Diemer, *Edmund Husserl* (Meisenheim am Glan, 1956), p. 30, footnote. The pagination is that of the first edition of *Sein und Zeit,* published in Volume VIII of the *Jahrbuch* (Halle, 1927).

ity." [4] Toward the end of the book, however, Husserl decides that Heidegger is done with phenomenology —that he sees no need to define, much less to warrant, his attitudes toward the phenomena which he chooses to investigate, i.e., no need to show what recommends them to his investigation. While Husserl did not himself claim much success in defining the proper attitudes and procedures of the philosophical inquirer, he felt that philosophy could not fulfill its "Cartesian mission" and become a science until such a definition, or at least the necessity for one, had been established. He talked with Heidegger at length of his misgivings, and Heidegger promised to answer them.

Soon after the appearance of *Sein und Zeit*, Husserl was commissioned to write an article on phenomenology for the *Encyclopaedia Britannica*. [5] Perhaps he saw in the article an opportunity to resolve his differences with Heidegger, for he asked him to collaborate, a rare gesture on his part. Heidegger never quite consented but, during a visit to Husserl's home in Freiburg, did work through the second

4. Husserl, on page 63: "Das ist in meinem Sinn der Weg zu einer intentionalen Psychologie der Personalität im weitesten Sinn von dem personalen Weltleben aus: ein fundierender personaler Typus."

5. Several drafts of the *Britannica* article appear in E. Husserl, *Phänomenologische Psychologie* (The Hague, 1962), pp. 237–301. Heidegger's revisions are included below the text of the second version; his letter appears in the Appendices, pp. 600–602. A translation of the article is reprinted from the 14th edition of the *Britannica* in R. Chisholm (ed.), *Realism and the Background of Phenomenology* (Glencoe, Ill., 1960). Cf. also W. Biemel, "Husserls Encyclopaedia-Britannica Artikel und Heideggers Anmerkungen dazu," *Tijdschrift voor Philosophie* (Louvain, 1950), Vol. XII.

draft. He later sent along his revisions with a covering note, which included the following observation:

> We agree that being [*das Seiende*], in the sense of that which you call the "world," cannot be clarified through a return to beings of the same nature. But this does not mean that what determines the location [*Ort*] of the transcendental is not a being at all. Rather it leads directly to the *problem:* What is the nature of being in which "world" is constituted? That is the central problem of *Sein und Zeit.* . . .[6]

While, in one way, the letter is a fair statement of their differences, it is quite misleading in another. For Heidegger certainly does not think that they agree about what must be called (the) "world." That is more like the issue on which their differences rest. It is enough of an issue that Heidegger can, and in *Vom Wesen des Grundes* does, argue that "the being in which the world is constituted," or Dasein, is rather of *exactly* the same nature as the world it constitutes. Which is to say, at the very least, that we should not think that it is clear what "world" means and unclear what "Dasein" means; we can be no clearer about one than we are about the other.

Vom Wesen des Grundes, despite its title, is largely concerned with the concept of "world," and in particular with establishing the concept's lineage —a legitimate concern, since the ordinary meanings of the term and Heidegger's are only oddly akin. The "world," on his definition, is not the "totality of

---

6. *Phänomenologische Psychologie*, p. 601. Husserl, at least, seems to have found the statement fair. He praised the letter and recopied Heidegger's remarks in shorthand, then had them entered in a carbon copy of the manuscript.

things" but that in terms of which we understand them, that which gives them measure and purpose and validity in our schemes. What leads Heidegger to offer the definition is not obvious, but it may well be related to explaining why we must, and no less how we *can*, share certain notions about the measure and purpose and validity of things. And presumably it is important to have that explanation because sometimes we *do not*, or do not seem to, share such notions.

Where Heidegger talks about "world," he will often appear to be talking about a pervasive interpretation or point of view which we bring to the things of the world. This, in any case, has been the view of many commentators. But there is little sense in speaking of "a point of view" here since precisely what Heidegger wants to indicate with the concept is that none other is possible. And there is no more sense in speaking of an interpretation when, instead of an interpretation, the "world" is meant to be that which can keep us from seeing, or force us to see, that what we have *is* one. Heidegger's concept is quite like Kierkegaard's "sphere of existence" and Wittgenstein's "form of life," and, as with them, it enters his inquiry only at its limits, when a problem moves out of his depth, or jurisdiction.

There is a way in which one cannot agree with Heidegger "on certain points" any more than one can, even in a manner of speaking, be insane or revolutionary on certain points. None of his concepts, the concept of world included, can be understood until one knows how to turn all of them to account. Until then, it is confusing how one goes about understanding him or, rather, how one decides *when* one

has understood him and *whether* one has understood him as others must. Our confusion is not anarchic; it has its own discipline. We are not, for example, concerned to ask whether his remarks are true; each will be an untried example of its own truth, a truth which one does not know how to fix. Nor are we concerned to examine certain new facts of his and their implications. For, though he is telling us something that we can have failed to know, he is not claiming to give us either additional or different information; the right preface for his remarks would not be "furthermore" or "on the other hand." We have a different interest, at the outset. We want to know the kind of *advantage* that Heidegger has over us in deciding what to say about Dasein or "world," e.g., the kind of precautions we might be expected to take before challenging Heidegger's own statement on the matter and whether a *challenge* is possible in the first place. It might appear that the only terms on which we could raise a challenge, or even voice our confusion, are either outlawed or do not begin to threaten his own; we cannot speak against Heidegger's terms, while, on them, we set no limit to his advantage; our challenge, then, would serve to discredit, not Heidegger, but our understanding of him. This may or may not be true. It is put forward as an example of what would settle the question of our relationship to Heidegger. And only if we know how we stand related to him will we also know what to *make of* our confusion.

But it is not as if Heidegger did not realize all this, or did and were satisfied with himself nonetheless. He is constantly aware of how far he is from making a case; he takes pains to assess his distance

and its consequences for him. Indeed, the analysis and treatment of his failure to make a case are as internal to his work, and often as thematic,[7] as his more obscure exercises with the notion of Dasein. Perhaps the *reasons* which he gives for his failure are wrong, but there is nothing wrong, no necessary finality, in his failure as such; or, if there is, then it is at least unclear who is in the wrong.

Our problems are problems with Heidegger's language. What gives them their force as problems is that they ask to be solved in and through his language, without further recourse. Heidegger is not, certainly by his own account, using new and peculiar words as "equivalents" for our own, and, even if he were, there is no reason to think that we would then be in some better position to understand him. Which is to say that the difficulty is not one of *decoding* him, as, we have seen, Husserl believed for a while. If Heidegger resorts to his own peculiar language, it is because ordinary German does not meet his purposes; and it does not because he has new and different purposes. If we cannot educate ourselves to his purposes, then clearly his work will look like nonsense. And yet we should not conclude that it *is* nonsense merely because we are not sure what is to keep us from the conclusion.

When it comes to divining Heidegger's purposes, his arguments and descriptions will not be very helpful, or will only help and fail to help in the manner of, for example, the exegesis of a religious text. They are not strictly arguments or descriptions, one sus-

7. One need only look at the Introduction to *Sein und Zeit* or the discussion of "ordinariness" (*Alltäglichkeit*) in §§ 35–38.

pects, but are designed to make such procedures, and the proper application of them, possible. They assume that we have learned where to look for their relevances—that, paradoxically, we have already gained the "horizon" which *Sein und Zeit* set out to *open* for us, namely, the "transcendental horizon of the question about Being"—and that, insofar as we have, we *necessarily* share his purposes and need not depend on his arguments.

Aside from helping the reader with the German, little is left to the translator. There are a number of more or less inevitable mistakes and inadequacies in the translation, inevitable in the sense that no gloss or paraphrase could mitigate them or could make other phrasings look like alternatives. The translator must be content with the thought that he will have succeeded, in a way, if such mistakes can become important in the first place, since the reader will be only as vulnerable to them as he is alive to Heidegger's inventions.

The Essence of Reasons
Vom Wesen des Grundes

VORWORT ZUR DRITTEN AUFLAGE

DIE ABHANDLUNG »*Vom Wesen des Grundes*« *entstand im Jahre 1928 gleichzeitig mit der Vorlesung* »*Was ist Metaphysik?*«. *Diese bedenkt das Nichts, jene nennt die ontologische Differenz.*

Das Nichts ist das Nicht des Seienden und so das vom Seienden her erfahrene Sein. Die ontologische Differenz ist das Nicht zwischen Seiendem und Sein. Aber sowenig Sein als das Nicht zum Seienden ein Nichts ist im Sinne des nihil negativum, sowenig ist die Differenz als das Nicht zwischen Seiendem und Sein nur das Gebilde einer Distinktion des Verstandes (ens rationis).

Jenes nichtende Nicht des Nichts und dieses nichtende Nicht der Differenz sind zwar nicht einerlei, aber das Selbe im Sinne dessen, was im Wesenden des Seins des Seienden zusammengehört. Dieses Selbe ist das Denkwürdige, das beide mit Absicht getrennt gehaltenen Schriften einer Besinnung näher zu bringen versuchen, ohne dieser gewachsen zu sein.

Wie wäre es, wenn die Besinnlichen begännen, auf diese seit zwei Jahrzehnten wartende selbe Sache endlich denkend einzugehen?

Preface to the Third Edition (1949)

THE TREATISE The Essence of Reasons *was written in 1928, at the same time as the lecture* What is Metaphysics? *The latter considers the problem of Nothingness, while the former defines the Ontological Difference.*

Nothingness is the Not of being and thus is Being experienced from the point of view of being. The Ontological Difference [1] * is the Not between being and Being. Yet Being, as the Not to being, is no more a nothingness in the sense of a nihil negativum *than the Difference, as the Not between being and Being, is merely a distinction of the intellect* (ens rationis).

The nihilating Not of Nothingness and the nihilating Not of the Difference are not, indeed, identical. But they are the same in the sense that both belong together insofar as the Being of being reveals its essence. [2] This sameness is a matter which merits thought and which the two works, purposely kept separate, attempt to consider more closely, though neither is equal to the task.

Why shouldn't considerate minds finally begin to look thoughtfully into this matter, which has been awaiting their attention for two decades?

---

* Numbers in brackets refer to the translator's Critical Notes, which begin on page 133, and bracketed words in the text are his insertions, not the author's.

ARISTOTELES faßt seine Auseinanderlegung der mannigfachen Bedeutungen des Wortes ἀρχή also zusammen: πασῶν μὲν οὖν κοινὸν τῶν ἀρχῶν τὸ πρῶτον εἶναι ὅθεν ἢ ἔστιν ἢ γίγνεται ἢ γιγνώσκεται.[1] Hiermit sind die Abwandlungen dessen herausgehoben, was wir »Grund« zu nennen pflegen: der Grund des Was-seins, des Daß-seins und des Wahr-seins. Darüber hinaus aber wird noch das zu fassen gesucht, worin diese »Gründe« als solche übereinkommen. Ihr κοινόν ist τὸ πρῶτον ὅθεν, das Erste, von wo aus . . . Neben dieser dreifachen Gliederung der obersten »Anfänge« findet sich eine Vierteilung des αἴτιον (»Ursache«) in ὑποκείμενον, τὸ τί ἦν εἶναι, ἀρχὴ τῆς μεταβολῆς und οὗ ἕνεκα,[2] die in der nachkommenden Geschichte der »Metaphysik« und »Logik« leitend geblieben ist. Obzwar πάντα τὰ αἴτια für ἀρχαί erkannt werden, der innere Zusammenhang zwischen den Einteilungen und ihr Prinzip bleiben im Dunkel. Und ob gar das Wesen des Grundes gefunden wer-

1. Metaphysik Δ 1, 1013 a 17 sqq.
2. A. a. O. Δ 2, 1013 b 16 sqq.

ARISTOTLE sums up his analysis of the several meanings of the word "beginning" as follows: "It is common, then, to all beginnings to be the first point from which a thing either is, or comes to be, or is known." [1] Here we find an account of the various kinds of what we commonly call "reasons" or "grounds": the reason for what a being is, for the fact that it is, and for its being true. [3] Aristotle also tries to determine in what respect these "reasons" agree with one another. Their "common property" lies in their being "the first point from which. . . ." Along with this threefold classification of supreme "beginnings," we find a fourfold division of "causes" into "material," "formal," "efficient," and "final" [2]—a division that assumed a prominent role in the subsequent history of "metaphysics" and "logic." Although Aristotle recognizes "all the causes" for "beginnings," the inner connection between each of the divisions and its principle remains obscure. Moreover, it is doubtful whether one can

1. *Metaphysics* Δ 1, 1013a, 17 ff.
2. *Metaphysics* Δ 2, 1013b, 16 ff.

[5]

den kann auf dem Wege einer Kennzeichnung dessen, was den »Arten« von Gründen »gemeinsam«
ist, muß bezweifelt werden, wenngleich darin der
Zug zu einer ursprünglichen Erhellung von Grund
überhaupt nicht verkannt werden darf. *Aristoteles*
hat sich auch nicht bei den »vier Ursachen« als nur
aufgerafften beruhigt, sondern sich um ein Verständnis ihres Zusammenhangs und eine Begründung der Vierzahl bemüht. Das verrät sowohl deren
ausführliche Analyse in Physik B als vor allem auch
die »problemgeschichtliche« Erörterung der Frage
nach den »vier Ursachen« in Metaphysik A 3–7, die
Aristoteles mit der Feststellung schließt: ὅτι μὲν οὖν
ὀρθῶς διώρισται περὶ τῶν αἰτίων καὶ πόσα καὶ ποῖα, μαρτυρεῖν
ἐοίκασιν ἡμῖν καὶ οὗτοι πάντες, οὐ δυνάμενοι θιγεῖν ἄλλης αἰτίας,
πρὸς δὲ τούτοις ὅτι ζητητέαι αἱ ἀρχαὶ ἢ οὕτως ἅπασαι ἢ τινὰ
τρόπον τοιοῦτον δῆλον.[3] Die vor- und imgleichen die
nacharistotelische Geschichte des Problems des
Grundes muß hier wegfallen. Im Hinblick auf die
geplante Ansetzung des Problems sei jedoch an
Folgendes erinnert. Durch *Leibniz* ist das Problem
des Grundes in der Gestalt der Frage nach dem
principium rationis sufficientis bekannt. Monogra-
phisch hat erstmals *Chr. A. Crusius* den »Satz vom
Grunde« in seiner Dissertatio philosophica de usu et
limitibus principii rationis determinantis vulgo sufficientis (1743)[4] behandelt und zuletzt *Schopen-*

---

3. Metaphysik A 7, 988 b 16 sqq.
4. Vgl. Opuscula philosophico-theologica antea seorsum
edita nunc secundis curis revisa et copiose aucta. Lipsiae
1750, p. 152 sqq.

get at the essence of reasons by characterizing what is "common" to the various "kinds" of reasons, even though doing so might undeniably bring one closer to a preliminary clarification of reasons. Aristotle himself was not content to single out the "four causes" and leave the matter there, but strove to understand how they are interrelated and to prove why they are four in number. That this was his aim is indicated in his detailed analysis of the causes in *Physics* B and even more clearly in his discussion of the whole question about the "four causes" in the light of the "history of the problem," which we find in *Metaphysics* A 3–7, and which Aristotle concludes with the statement: "All these thinkers, then, as they cannot find another cause, seem to be saying that we have correctly established both how many and of what kind the causes are. Aside from this it is clear that when the causes are being sought, either all four must be sought thus or they must be sought in one of these ways." [3] The history of the problem of reasons, both before and since Aristotle, cannot be considered here. But since we plan to address ourselves to the problem eventually, we would do well to bear the following in mind. Thanks to Leibniz, the problem of reasons is known in the form of the question about the *principium rationis sufficientis*. The "principle of sufficient reason" [4] was first treated at length in Christian A. Crusius' monograph, *Philosophical Dissertation Concerning the Use and Limits of the Principle of Determinative and Commonly Sufficient Reason* (1743),[4] and last

3. *Metaphysics* A 7, 988b, 16 ff.
4. Cf. *Opuscula philosophico-theologica antea seorsum edita nunc secundis curis revisa et copiose aucta* (Leipzig, 1750), pp. 152 ff.

hauer in seiner Dissertation »Über die vierfache Wurzel des Satzes vom zureichenden Grunde« (1813).[5] Wenn aber das Problem des Grundes mit den Kernfragen der Metaphysik überhaupt verklammert ist, dann muß es auch dort lebendig sein, wo es nicht ausdrücklich in der bekannten Gestalt abgehandelt wird. So hat *Kant* scheinbar dem »Satz vom Grunde« ein geringes Interesse entgegengebracht, wenn er ihn auch sowohl am Beginn [6] seines Philosophierens als auch gegen Ende [7] ausdrücklich erörtert. Und doch steht er im Zentrum der Kritik der reinen Vernunft.[8] Von nicht geringerer Bedeutung aber für das Problem sind *Schellings* »Philosophische Untersuchungen über das Wesen der menschlichen Freiheit und die damit zusammenhängenden Gegenstände« (1809).[9] Schon der Hinweis auf Kant und Schelling macht fraglich, ob sich das Problem des Grundes mit dem des »Satzes vom Grunde« deckt und ob es überhaupt mit diesem auch nur gestellt ist. Trifft das nicht zu, dann bedarf das Problem des Grundes erst einer Weckung, was nicht ausschließt, daß hierzu eine Erörterung des »Satzes vom Grunde« Veranlassung geben und erste Anweisung vermitteln kann. Die Auseinanderlegung des Problems aber ist gleichbedeutend mit der Gewinnung und Auszeichnung des *Bezirks,* innerhalb dessen *vom* Wesen des Grundes gehandelt werden soll ohne den Anspruch, dieses mit einem

5. 2. Aufl. 1847, 3. Aufl. hrsg. von Jul. Frauenstädt 1864.
6. Principiorum primorum cognitionis metaphysicae nova dilucidatio. 1755.
7. Über eine Entdeckung, nach der alle neue Kritik der reinen Vernunft durch eine ältere entbehrlich gemacht werden soll. 1790.
8. Vgl. unten S. 30.
9. WW. I. Abt., Bd. 7, S. 333–416.

in Schopenhauer's dissertation, *Concerning the Fourfold Root of the Principle of Sufficient Reason* (1813).[5] But if the problem of reasons is bound up with the central questions of metaphysics, then it must also arise even where it is not explicitly treated in its familiar form. Thus, though Kant discusses the "principle of sufficient reason" explicitly, both at the beginning,[6] as well as toward the end,[7] of his philosophizing, [5] he apparently regarded it with little interest. And yet it stands at the center of his *Critique of Pure Reason*.[8] No less relevant to the problem is Schelling's *Philosophical Investigations Concerning the Essence of Human Freedom and Pertinent Matters* (1809).[9] The reference to Kant and Schelling alone makes it questionable whether the problem of reasons coincides with that of the "principle of sufficient reason"—indeed whether the former is even raised by the latter at all. If it is not, then the problem of reasons must first be awakened, which does not exclude the possibility that a discussion [6] of the "principle of sufficient reason" can provide the occasion and initial direction for awakening the problem. To analyze the problem means to gain access to and mark out the *realm* within which we should treat the question *concerning* the essence of reasons—making no claim to expose it to view straightway. [7] This realm is shown to be the realm

5. 2d ed. (1847); 3d ed., edited by Julius Frauenstädt (1864).

6. *Principiorum primorum cognitionis metaphysicae nova dilucidatio* (1775).

7. *Über eine Entdeckung, nach der alle neue Kritik der reinen Vernunft durch eine ältere entbehrlich gemacht werden soll* (1790).

8. Cf. below, p. 31.

9. *Sämmtliche Werke*, edited by K. F. A. Schelling (1860), Vol. VII, Part I, pp. 333–416.

Schlag vor Augen legen zu wollen. Als dieser Bezirk wird die *Transzendenz* herausgestellt. Das sagt zugleich: sie wird durch das Problem des Grundes gerade erst selbst ursprünglicher und umfassender bestimmt. Alle Wesenserhellung muß als *philosophierende,* d. h. als eine zu innerst *endliche* Anstrengung immer auch notwendig für das *Unwesen* zeugen, das *menschliche* Erkenntnis mit allem Wesen treibt. Somit hat sich die Gliederung des Folgenden ergeben: I. Das Problem des Grundes; II. die Transzendenz als Bezirk der Frage nach dem Wesen des Grundes; III. Vom Wesen des Grundes.

I / DAS PROBLEM DES GRUNDES

DER »SATZ VOM GRUNDE« scheint als ein »oberstes Prinzip« dergleichen wie ein *Problem* des Grundes von vornherein abzuwehren. Ist denn aber der »Satz des Grundes« eine Aussage *über* den Grund als solchen? Enthüllt er als oberster Satz gar das Wesen des Grundes? Die vulgäre und verkürzte Fassung des Satzes lautet: nihil est sine ratione, nichts ist ohne Grund. In der positiven Umschreibung sagt das: omne ens habet rationem, jedes Seiende hat einen Grund. Der Satz sagt *über das Seiende* aus und das aus der Hinblicknahme auf so etwas wie »Grund«. Was jedoch das Wesen von Grund ausmacht, wird *in* diesem Satz nicht bestimmt. Das ist *für* diesen Satz als eine selbstverständliche »Vorstellung« vorausgesetzt. Der »oberste« Satz vom Grunde macht aber noch in anderer Weise vom *ungeklärten* Wesen des Grundes Ge-

of *transcendence*. That is to say: transcendence is itself primordially and comprehensively defined through the problem of reasons. As a way of *philosophizing,* and so as a basically *finite* enterprise, the effort to illuminate any essence reflects the *confusion* that *human* knowledge breeds with every essence. [8] Thus the present work falls into the following divisions: I. The Problem of Reasons, II. Transcendence as the Realm of the Question about the Essence of Reasons, and III. The Essence of Reasons.

I / THE PROBLEM OF REASONS

AS A "SUPREME PRINCIPLE," the "principle of sufficient reason" seems, from the outset, to obviate anything like a *problem* of reasons. But does the "principle of sufficient reason" represent a statement *about* reasons as such? As a supreme principle, does it in any way reveal the essence of reasons? The popular, abbreviated version of the principle runs: *nihil est sine ratione,* "nothing is without reason." Stated positively, this reads: *omne ens habet rationem,* "every being has a reason." The principle states something *about being* with reference to something called a "reason." Yet what constitutes the essence of reasons is not specified *in* this principle. It is presupposed *by* this principle as a "notion" that is obvious to everyone. [9] The "supreme" [10] principle of sufficient reason makes use of the *unclarified* essence of reasons in yet another way; the unique propositional character of this

brauch; denn der spezifische Satzcharakter dieses
Satzes als eines »Grund«-satzes, das Prinziphafte
dieses principium grande (Leibniz) läßt sich ursprünglich doch nur im Hinblick auf das Wesen von
Grund umgrenzen.

So ist der »Satz vom Grunde« sowohl in seiner
Setzungsweise als auch in dem von ihm gesetzten
»Gehalt« fragwürdig, wenn anders das Wesen von
Grund über eine unbestimmt allgemeine »Vorstel-
lung« hinaus Problem werden kann und soll.

Wenn der Satz vom Grunde gleich über den
Grund als solchen keine Aufhellung gibt, so kann
er doch zum Ausgang einer Kennzeichnung des
Problems des Grundes dienen. Freilich unterliegt
der Satz—von den genannten Fragwürdigkeiten
noch ganz abgesehen—mannigfachen Deutungen
und Einschätzungen. Für die jetzige Absicht liegt es
jedoch nahe, den Satz in der Fassung und Rolle
aufzunehmen, die ihm erstmals *Leibniz* ausdrücklich gegeben hat. Aber gerade hier ist umstritten,
ob das principium rationis für *Leibniz* als ein »logi-
sches« oder ein »metaphysisches« oder als beides
gelte. Solange wir uns freilich eingestehen, weder
vom Begriff der »Logik« noch von dem der »Metaphysik« noch gar vom »Verhältnis« beider etwas
Rechtes zu wissen, bleiben die Streitigkeiten der
historischen Leibnizauslegung ohne sicheren Leitfaden und daher philosophisch unfruchtbar. Keines-
falls können sie das beeinträchtigen, was im Folgenden über das principium rationis aus *Leibniz*
beigezogen wird. Es genüge die Anführung einer
Hauptstelle aus dem Traktat »Primae veritates«: [10]

10. Vgl. Opuscules et fragments inédits de Leibniz ed.
L. Couturat, 1903, p. 518 sqq. Vgl. auch Revue de Métaphysique et de Morale, t. X (1902), p. 2 sqq.—Couturat

proposition as a basic proposition, that which characterizes this *principium grande* (Leibniz) as a principle, ultimately can be defined only with reference to the essence of reasons.

Thus the "principle of sufficient reason" raises questions regarding both the manner in which it is advanced and its "content"—at least if we grant that the essence of reasons can and should become a problem, and so more than a vaguely general "notion."

Though the principle of sufficient reason sheds no light on reasons as such, it can nevertheless serve as our point of departure in characterizing the problem of reasons. Of course the principle may—disregarding the above difficulties—be interpreted and evaluated in many ways. For our present purposes, however, we would do best to take it up in the version and role that Leibniz was the first to give it explicitly. But here there has been debate. At issue is whether Leibniz considers the *principium rationis* a "logical" principle, a "metaphysical" principle, or both. [11] As long as we admit that we know nothing precise about either the concept of "logic" or the concept of "metaphysics" or even about the "relationship" between the two, any debate over the historiological interpretation of Leibniz will remain unguided and so philosophically unfruitful. It cannot, in any case, undermine Leibniz' following argument about the *principium rationis*. To render the argument, it will be enough to quote an important passage from the treatise *First Truths:* [10]

10. Cf. *Opuscules et fragments inédits de Leibniz,* edited by L. Couturat (1903), pp. 518 ff. Cf. also *Revue de métaphysique et de morale,* X (1902), 2 ff. Couturat gives special weight to this treatise, because it supposedly provides

Semper igitur praedicatum seu consequens inest subjecto seu antecedenti; et in hoc ipso consistit natura veritatis in universum seu connexio inter terminos enuntiationis, ut etiam Aristoteles observavit. Et in identicis quidem connexio illa atque comprehensio praedicati in subjecto est expressa, in reliquis omnibus implicita, ac per analysin notionum ostendenda, in qua demonstratio a priori sita est.

Hoc autem verum est in omni veritate affirmativa universali aut singulari, necessaria aut contingente, et in denominatione tam intrinseca quam extrinseca. Et latet hic arcanum mirabile a quo natura contingentiae seu essentiale discrimen veritatum necessariarum et contingentium continetur, et difficultas de fatali rerum etiam liberarum necessitate tollitur.

Ex his propter nimiam facilitatem suam non satis consideratis multa consequuntur magni momenti. Statim enim hinc nascitur axioma receptum, *nihil esse sine ratione,* seu *nullum effectum esse absque causa.* Alioqui veritas daretur, quae non potest probari a priori, seu quae non resolveretur in identicas, quod est contra naturam veritatis, quae semper vel expresse vel implicite identica est.

---

weist diesem Traktat eine besondere Bedeutung zu, weil er ihm einen schlagenden Beweis für seine These liefern soll, que la métaphysique de Leibniz repose toute entière sur la logique. Wenn dieser Traktat den folgenden Erörterungen zugrunde gelegt wird, so ist das keine Zustimmung weder zu C.s Interpretation desselben, noch zu seiner Leibnizauffassung überhaupt, noch gar zu seinem Begriff der Logik. Dieser Traktat spricht vielmehr am schärfsten *gegen* den Ursprung des principium rationis aus der Logik, ja überhaupt *gegen* die Fragestellung, ob bei Leibniz der Logik oder der Metaphysik der Vorrang gebühre. Eine solche Fragemöglichkeit kommt gerade durch *Leibniz* ins Wanken und erfährt durch *Kant* eine erste, wenngleich nicht weiterwirkende Erschütterung.

Thus a predicate, or consequent, is always present in a subject, or antecedent; and in this fact consists the universal nature of truth, or the connection between the terms of the assertion, as Aristotle has also observed. This connection and inclusion of the predicate in the subject is explicit in relations of identity. In all other relations it is implicit and is revealed through an analysis of notions, upon which *a priori* demonstration is based.

The above holds true for every affirmative truth, whether universal or singular, necessary or contingent, as well as for both intrinsic and extrinsic denomination. This wondrous secret goes unnoticed, this secret which reveals the nature of contingency, or the essential distinction between necessary and contingent truths, and which even removes the difficulty regarding the inevitable necessity of free beings.

From these things, which have not been adequately considered due to their great simplicity, there follow many other things of great importance. Indeed, from them there at once arises the familiar axiom: "Nothing is without reason," or "there is no effect without a cause." If the axiom did not hold, there might be a truth which could not be proved *a priori*, i.e., which could not be resolved into relations of identity; and this is contrary to the nature of truth, which is always identical, whether explicitly or implicitly.

---

him with striking proof for his thesis that "the metaphysics of Leibniz rests wholly on his logic." Though the treatise lies at the basis of the following discussion, this implies no agreement either with Couturat's interpretation of it or with his views on Leibniz generally or, for that matter, with his concept of logic. The treatise tells quite pointedly against placing the origin of the *principium rationis* in logic and even against posing the question of whether Leibniz awards logic or metaphysics a priority. Leibniz was the first to set the possibility of such a question in doubt; Kant gave it an initial jolt, but the effect did not last.

Leibniz gibt hier nach einer für ihn charakteristischen Weise *in eins* mit der Kennzeichnung der »*ersten* Wahrheiten« eine Bestimmung dessen, was Wahrheit *erstlich* und überhaupt ist und zwar in der Absicht, die »Geburt« des principium rationis aus der natura veritatis zu zeigen. Und gerade bei diesem Unternehmen hält er für nötig darauf hinzuweisen, daß die scheinbare Selbstverständlichkeit solcher Begriffe wie »Wahrheit«, »Identität« eine Klärung derselben hintanhalte, die hinreiche, den Ursprung des principium rationis und der übrigen Axiome darzutun. Für die vorliegende Betrachtung steht aber nicht die Ableitung des principium rationis in Frage, sondern die Auseinanderlegung des Problems des Grundes. Inwiefern bietet die angezogene Stelle hierzu einen Leitfaden?

Das principium rationis besteht, weil ohne seinen Bestand Seiendes wäre, was grundlos sein müßte. Für *Leibniz* heißt das: es gäbe Wahres, das sich einer Auflösung in Identitäten widersetzte, es gäbe Wahrheiten, die gegen die »Natur« von Wahrheit überhaupt verstoßen müßten. Weil das jedoch unmöglich ist und Wahrheit besteht, deshalb hat auch das principium rationis, weil aus dem Wesen der Wahrheit entspringend, Bestand. Das Wesen der Wahrheit aber liegt in der connexio (συμπλοκή) von Subjekt und Prädikat. *Leibniz* faßt demnach die Wahrheit von vornherein und mit ausdrücklicher, obzwar nicht berechtigter Berufung auf *Aristoteles* als Aussage-(Satz)wahrheit. Den nexus bestimmt er als »inesse« des P in S, das »inesse« aber als »idem esse«. Identität als Wesen der Satzwahrheit besagt hier offenbar nicht leere Selbigkeit von etwas mit sich selbst, sondern Einheit

Here, bound up with his characterization of *"first* truths," Leibniz characteristically gives a definition of what truth is *firstly* and in general. He hopes thereby to demonstrate that the *principium rationis* is "born" in and from the *natura veritatis.* For the success of his demonstration, he thinks it is necessary to point out that the apparent self-evidence of such concepts as "truth" and "identity" hinders the kind of clarification of them that would adequately set forth the origin of the *principium rationis* and the other axioms. But what now stands in question is not the derivation of the *principium rationis* but the analysis of the problem of reasons. To what extent does the passage quoted above offer us some clue in this analysis?

The *principium rationis* exists because, if it did not, there would be beings which would necessarily be without reason. For Leibniz, this means that there would be truths which resisted resolution into relations of identity; there would be truths, that is, which would necessarily run counter to the "nature" of truth in general. Because this is impossible, because there is such a thing as truth, there is also such a thing as the *principium rationis.* For the principle arises from the essence of truth. But, the argument continues, the essence of truth lies in the *connexio* (*symplokē*) of subject and predicate. Thus, with explicit though unjustified reference to Aristotle, Leibniz begins by construing truth as truth of the assertion (proposition). He then defines the nexus of subject and predicate as the *"inesse"* of the predicate in the subject, but he goes on to define this *"inesse"* as *"idem esse."* Here "identity," as the essence of propositional truth, obviously does not mean

im Sinne der ursprünglichen Einigkeit des Zusammengehörigen. Wahrheit bedeutet demnach Einstimmigkeit, die ihrerseits solche nur ist als Übereinstimmung mit dem, was sich in der Identität als Einiges bekundet. Die »Wahrheiten«—wahre Aussagen—nehmen ihrer Natur nach Bezug zu etwas, *auf Grund wovon* sie Einstimmigkeiten sein können. Das auseinanderlegende Verknüpfen in jeder Wahrheit ist, was es ist, je immer auf Grund von . . . , d. h. als sich »begründendes«. Der *Wahrheit* wohnt demnach ein wesensmäßiger Bezug inne zu dergleichen wie »Grund«. Dann bringt aber das Problem der Wahrheit notwendig in die »Nähe« des Problems des Grundes. Je ursprünglicher wir uns daher des Wesens der Wahrheit bemächtigen, um so aufdringlicher muß das Problem des Grundes werden.

Läßt sich jedoch über die Umgrenzung des Wesens der Wahrheit als Charakter der Aussage hinaus noch Ursprünglicheres beibringen? Nichts weniger als die Einsicht, daß diese Wesensbestimmung der Wahrheit—wie immer sie im einzelnen gefaßt sein mag—eine zwar unumgängliche aber gleichwohl abgeleitete ist.[11] Die Übereinstimmung des nexus *mit* dem Seienden und ihr zufolge seine Einstimmigkeit machen *als solche* nicht primär das Seiende zugänglich. Dieses muß vielmehr als das mögliche Worüber einer prädikativen Bestimmung *vor* dieser Prädikation und *für* sie schon offenbar sein. Prädikation muß, um möglich zu werden, sich

11. Vgl. M. *Heidegger*, Sein und Zeit I, 1927 (Jahrbuch für Philosophie und phänomenologische Forschung, Bd. VIII), § 44, S. 212–230; über die Aussage § 33, S. 154 ff.— Die Seitenzahlen stimmen mit denen des Sonderdruckes überein.

any empty sameness of something with itself but "unity" in the sense of the original oneness of that which belongs together. Truth, then, means consonance. And consonance is only "consonance" as correspondence with that which announces itself as "at one" or "alike" in the identity. [12] By their very nature, "truths," i.e., true assertions, refer to something *by reason of which* they can be consonant. The dividing connecting in every truth is what it is only "by reason of . . . ," i.e., as a connecting that "founds" itself. Thus an essential relationship to something like "reasons" dwells at the very heart of *truth*. The problem of truth now enters the "neighborhood" of the problem of reasons. The more originally we seize upon the problem of the essence of truth, therefore, the more persistent must the problem of reasons become.

Can we add something more original, something that goes beyond the definition of the essence of truth as a character of the assertion? Nothing less than the insight that this definition, however construed, is, though unavoidable, nonetheless derivative.[11] The correspondence of the nexus *with* being and its resulting consonance do not *as such* render being immediately accessible. Rather, as the possible "subject" of a predicative definition, being must already be manifest both *prior to* and *for* our predications. Predication, to become possible, must be able to establish itself in the sort of manifesting which does *not* have a *predicative* character. Propositional

11. Cf. M. Heidegger, "Sein und Zeit," Part I, § 44, in *Jahrbuch für Philosophie und phänomenologische Forschung,* VIII (1927), 212–30; concerning "assertions" cf. § 33, pp. 154 ff. The page numbers correspond to those of the special edition.

in einem Offenbarmachen ansiedeln können, das *nicht prädikativen* Charakter hat. Die Satzwahrheit ist in einer *ursprünglicheren* Wahrheit (Unverborgenheit), in der vorprädikativen Offenbarkeit *von Seiendem* gewurzelt, die *ontische Wahrheit* genannt sei. Den verschiedenen Arten und Bezirken des Seienden gemäß wandelt sich der Charakter seiner möglichen Offenbarkeit und der zugehörigen Weisen des auslegenden Bestimmens. So unterscheidet sich z. B. die Wahrheit von Vorhandenem (z. B. der materiellen Dinge) als *Entdecktheit* spezifisch von der Wahrheit des Seienden, das wir selbst sind, der *Erschlossenheit* des existierenden Daseins.[12] So vielfältig aber die Unterschiede dieser beiden Arten ontischer Wahrheit sein mögen, für alle vorprädikative Offenbarkeit gilt, daß das Offenbarmachen *primär* nie den Charakter eines bloßen Vorstellens (Anschauens) hat, selbst nicht in der »ästhetischen« Betrachtung. Die Kennzeichnung der vorprädikativen Wahrheit als Anschauen legt sich *deshalb* gern nahe, weil die ontische und vermeintlich eigentliche Wahrheit zuvörderst als Satzwahrheit, d. i. als »*Vorstellungs-verbindung*« bestimmt wird. Das *dieser* gegenüber Einfachere ist dann ein verbindungsfreies, schlichtes Vorstellen. Dieses hat zwar für die *Vergegenständlichung* des freilich dann immer schon notwendig offenbaren Seienden seine eigene Funktion. Das ontische Offenbaren selbst aber geschieht im stimmungsmäßigen und triebhaften Sichbefinden[13] inmitten von Seiendem und in den hierin mitgegründeten strebensmäßigen und willentlichen Verhaltungen zum Seienden. Doch selbst diese vermöchten nicht, weder als vorprädi-

12. Vgl. a. a. O. § 60, S. 295 ff.
13. Über »Befindlichkeit« vgl. a. a. O. § 29, S. 134 ff.

truth is rooted in a *more primordial* truth (unconcealedness); it is rooted in that prepredicative manifestness *of being* which we call *ontical truth.* [13]
The character of its manifestness, and of the pertinent kinds of explanatory defining, varies with the
many kinds and realms of being. Thus, for example,
discoveredness, or the truth of that which is present
at hand (e.g., of material things), is uniquely different from the *disclosedness* of existing Dasein, or the
truth of the kind of being which we ourselves are.[12]
As numerous as the differences of these two kinds of
ontic truth may be, all prepredicative manifestness
is such that, at a *primary* level, manifesting never
has the character of a mere representing (intuiting), not even in "aesthetic" contemplation. We will
be inclined to characterize prepredicative truth as
intuiting *only if* ontic, and presumably authentic,
truth is defined as propositional truth, i.e., as a
"combination of representations." For the next most
simple thing to a "combination of representations"
is, indeed, a plain representing (one free from combination). The proper function of representing is to
objectivize being—which itself must then always be
already manifest. Ontical manifesting, however,
takes place in our situating ourselves [13] in the midst
of being, through our moods and drives, as well as
in the conative and volitional kinds of behavior toward being that are grounded in the way we find
ourselves situated. Yet even such behavior—whether
displayed in a prepredicative or a predicative manner—could not make beings accessible in themselves
were their manifesting not already guided and clarified by an understanding of the Being (the constitu-

12. Cf. *ibid.*, § 60, pp. 295 ff.
13. On "situatedness" cf. *ibid.*, § 29, pp. 134 ff.

kative noch als prädikativ sich auslegende, Seiendes
an ihm selbst zugänglich zu machen, wenn ihr
Offenbaren nicht schon immer zuvor erleuchtet und
geführt wäre durch ein Verständnis des Seins (Seinsverfassung: Was- und Wie-sein) des Seienden.
*Enthülltheit des Seins ermöglicht erst Offenbarkeit
von Seiendem.* Diese Enthülltheit als Wahrheit
über das Sein wird *ontologische Wahrheit* genannt.
Freilich sind die Termini »Ontologie« und »ontologisch« mehrdeutig, so zwar, daß sich gerade das
eigentümliche Problem einer Ontologie verbirgt.
Λόγος des ὄν heißt: das Ansprechen (λέγειν) des
Seienden als Seiendes, zugleich aber bedeutet es
das, *woraufhin* Seiendes angesprochen ist (λεγόμε-
νον). Etwas *als* etwas ansprechen besagt aber noch
nicht notwendig: das so Angesprochene *in seinem
Wesen begreifen.* Das alles Verhalten zu Seiendem
vorgängig erhellende und führende *Verstehen* des
Seins (λόγος in einer ganz weiten Bedeutung) ist
weder ein Erfassen des Seins als solchen, noch gar
ein Begreifen des so Erfaßten (λόγος in der engsten
Bedeutung = »ontologischer« Begriff). Das noch
nicht zum Begriff gekommene Seinsverständnis nennen wir daher das vor-ontologische oder auch das
ontologische im weiteren Sinne. Seinsbegreifen
setzt voraus, daß das Seinsverständnis sich selbst
ausgebildet und das in ihm verstandene, überhaupt
entworfene und irgendwie enthüllte Sein eigens
zum Thema und Problem gemacht hat. Zwischen
vorontologischem Seinsverständnis und ausdrücklicher Problematik des Seinsbegreifens gibt es viel-
fache Stufen. Eine charakteristische ist z. B. der
Entwurf der Seinsverfassung vom Seienden, durch
den zugleich ein bestimmtes Feld abgesteckt wird
(Natur, Geschichte) als Gebiet möglicher Vergegen-

tion of Being: what something is and how it is) of beings. *The disclosedness of Being alone makes possible the manifestness of being.* As the truth about Being, this disclosedness is called *ontological truth.* The terms "ontology" and "ontological" have so many meanings that they conceal the proper problem of an ontology. The *logos* of *on* means the addressing (*legein*) of beings as beings. But it also means that *to which* beings are addressed (*legomenon*). To address something *as* something does not necessarily mean to *grasp* that which is addressed *in its essence.* The *understanding* of Being (*logos* in a very broad sense), which from the outset clarifies and guides every way of behaving toward being, is neither a grasping of Being as such nor even a comprehending of that which is grasped (*logos* in the narrowest sense = "ontological" concept). The sort of understanding of Being that has not yet been conceptualized we call "preontological" or "ontological in the broader sense." In order to conceptualize Being, the understanding of Being must have developed of its own accord and have made Being (which is understood, generally projected, and somehow disclosed in it) its problem and theme of inquiry. There are many stages between the preontological understanding of Being and the explicit problematic involved in conceptualizing Being. One characteristic stage is the project of the constitution of the Being of being whereby a determinate field of being (perhaps nature or history) is, at the same time, marked off as an area that can be objectivized through scientific knowledge. The preliminary definition of the Being (understood here as what something is and how it is) of nature is established in the

ständlichung durch wissenschaftliche Erkenntnis. Die vorgängige Bestimmung des Seins (Was- und Wie-sein) von Natur überhaupt verfestigt sich in den »Grundbegriffen« der betreffenden Wissenschaft. In diesen Begriffen werden z. B. Raum, Ort, Zeit, Bewegung, Masse, Kraft, Geschwindigkeit umgrenzt, aber gleichwohl wird das Wesen von Zeit, Bewegung nicht eigenes Problem. Das Seinsverständnis des vorhandenen Seienden ist hier auf einen Begriff gebracht, allein die begriffliche Bestimmung von Zeit und Ort usf., die Definitionen, sind nach Ansatz und Reichweite einzig durch die Grundfragestellung geregelt, die in der betreffenden *Wissenschaft* an das Seiende ergeht. Die Grundbegriffe der heutigen Wissenschaft enthalten weder schon die »eigentlichen« ontologischen Begriffe des Seins des betreffenden Seienden, noch lassen sich diese lediglich durch eine »passende« Erweiterung jener gewinnen. Vielmehr müssen die ursprünglichen ontologischen Begriffe *vor* aller wissenschaftlichen Grundbegriffsdefinition gewonnen werden, so daß von ihnen aus allererst abschätzbar wird, in welcher einschränkenden und je aus einem bestimmten Blickpunkt umgrenzenden Weise die Grundbegriffe der Wissenschaften das in den rein ontologischen Begriffen faßbare Sein treffen. Das »Faktum« der Wissenschaften, d. h. der in ihnen notwendig so wie in jedem Verhalten zu Seiendem eingeschlossene faktische Bestand an Seinsverständnis ist weder Begründungsinstanz für das Apriori, noch die Quelle der Erkenntnis desselben, sondern nur eine mögliche veranlassende Anweisung auf die ursprüngliche Seinsverfassung z. B. von Geschichte oder Natur, eine Anweisung, die selbst noch der ständigen Kritik unterstellt bleiben muß, die ihre Richt-

"basic concepts" of natural science. Although space, locus, time, movement, mass, force, and velocity are defined in these concepts, the essence of time, movement, etc., does not become a problem in its own right. The understanding of the Being of what is present at hand is expressed conceptually here, but the application and scope of the conceptual definitions of time, locus, etc., are wholly determined by the basic inquiry to which being is submitted in natural *science.* The basic concepts of modern science do not include "authentic" ontological concepts of the Being of the being it treats, nor can the latter be obtained simply through a "suitable" extension of the former. Original ontological concepts must instead be obtained *prior* to any scientific definition of "basic concepts," so that only by proceeding from them will we be in a position to evaluate the manner in which the basic concepts of the sciences apply to Being as graspable in purely ontological concepts. The manner in which ontological concepts apply to Being will always be limited to and circumscribed by a definite point of view. The "fact" of the sciences, i.e., the factical [14] constituent of the understanding of Being that is necessarily included in them as in every way of behaving toward being, is neither a tribunal for founding the *a priori* nor the source of our knowledge of the *a priori* but merely a possible clue to the primordial constitution of the Being of, for example, history or nature. It is a clue which must itself be constantly subjected to the sort of criticism that has already gotten its bearings in the fundamental problematic of all inquiry about the Being of being.

punkte schon in der grundsätzlichen Problematik
alles Fragens nach dem Sein von Seiendem genommen hat.

Die möglichen Stufen und Abwandlungen der
ontologischen Wahrheit im weiteren Sinne verraten
zugleich den Reichtum dessen, was als ursprüngliche Wahrheit aller ontischen zugrunde liegt.[14]
Unverborgenheit des Seins aber ist immer Wahrheit
des Seins *von* Seiendem, mag dieses wirklich sein
oder nicht. Umgekehrt liegt in der Unverborgenheit
von Seiendem je schon eine solche seines Seins.
Ontische und ontologische Wahrheit betreffen je
verschieden *Seiendes in* seinem Sein und *Sein von*
Seiendem. Sie gehören wesenhaft zusammen auf
Grund ihres Bezugs zum *Unterschied von Sein und
Seiendem* (ontologische Differenz). Das dergestalt
notwendig ontisch-ontologisch gegabelte Wesen von
Wahrheit überhaupt ist nur möglich in eins mit
dem Aufbrechen dieses Unterschiedes. Wenn anders
nun das Auszeichnende des Daseins darin liegt,

14. Wenn man heute »Ontologie« und »ontologisch« als
Schlagwort und Titel für Richtungen in Anspruch nimmt,
dann sind diese Ausdrücke recht äußerlich und unter
Verkennung jeglicher Problematik gebraucht. Man lebt der
irrigen Meinung, Ontologie als Frage nach dem Sein des
Seienden bedeute »realistische« (naive oder kritische) »Ein-
stellung« gegenüber der »idealistischen«. Ontologische Problematik hat so wenig mit »Realismus« zu tun, daß gerade
Kant in und mit seiner *transzendentalen* Fragestellung den
ersten entscheidenden Schritt seit *Plato* und *Aristoteles* zu
einer *ausdrücklichen* Grundlegung der Ontologie vollziehen
konnte. Dadurch, daß man für die »Realität der Außenwelt«
eintritt, ist man noch nicht ontologisch orientiert. »Ontologisch«—in der populär-philosophischen Bedeutung genommen—meint jedoch—und darin bekundet sich die heillose
Verwirrung—das, was vielmehr ontisch genannt werden
muß, d. h. eine Haltung, die das *Seiende* an ihm selbst sein
läßt, was und wie es ist. Aber damit ist noch kein *Problem
des Seins* gestellt, geschweige denn das Fundament für die
Möglichkeit einer Ontologie gewonnen.

The several possible levels and varieties of ontological truth in the broader sense reveal the richness
of that which, as primordial truth, lies at the basis
of all ontical truth.[14] The unconcealedness [15] of
Being is the truth of the Being *of* being, whether or
not the latter is real. In the unconcealedness of
being, on the other hand, lies a prior unconcealedness of its Being. Each after its own fashion, ontical
and ontological truth concern *being in* its Being and
the *Being of* being. They belong together essentially,
by reason of their relationship to the *difference between Being and being* (the Ontological Difference). The essence of truth, which is and must be
bifurcated ontically and ontologically, is only possible given this difference. Yet if what is distinctive
about Dasein is that it behaves toward being by
understanding Being, then *the* ability to differen-
tiate the two (in which the Ontological Difference
becomes factical) must have struck the roots of its

14. Today people enlist the terms "ontology" and "ontological" as catchwords and labels for philosophical move-
ments; the expressions are used quite superficially and with
a lack of appreciation for everything problematical. People
work on the false assumption that ontology, as the question
about the Being of being, calls for a "standpoint" that is
"realistic" (naïve or critical) as opposed to one that is
"idealistic." An ontological problematic has little to do with
"realism," so little that it was only Kant, in and with his
transcendental method of inquiry, who could make the first
decisive step since Plato and Aristotle toward an *explicit*
founding of ontology. [16] Championing the "reality of the
external world" will not orient us ontologically. In its popular philosophical sense, "ontological" means (and here the
confusion becomes hopeless) something which should instead be called "ontical," i.e., an attitude which lets *being*
in itself be what and how it is. The *problem of Being* is not
posed, let alone the foundation for the possibility of an
ontology laid.

daß es Sein-verstehend zu Seiendem sich verhält, dann muß *das* Unterscheidenkönnen, in dem die ontologische Differenz faktisch wird, die Wurzel seiner eigenen Möglichkeit im Grunde des Wesens des Daseins geschlagen haben. Diesen Grund der ontologischen Differenz nennen wir vorgreifend die *Transzendenz* des Daseins.

Kennzeichnet man alles *Verhalten* zu Seiendem als intentionales, dann ist die *Intentionalität* nur möglich *auf dem Grunde der Transzendenz,* aber weder mit dieser identisch noch gar umgekehrt selbst die Ermöglichung der Transzendenz.[15]

Bisher galt es nur, in wenigen aber wesentlichen Schritten zu zeigen, daß das Wesen der Wahrheit ursprünglicher gesucht werden muß als die traditionelle Kennzeichnung dieser im Sinne einer Eigenschaft von Aussagen zulassen möchte. Wenn aber das Wesen des Grundes einen inneren Bezug zum Wesen der Wahrheit hat, dann kann auch das *Problem* des Grundes nur dort beheimatet sein, wo das Wesen der Wahrheit seine innere Möglichkeit schöpft, im Wesen der Transzendenz. Die Frage nach dem Wesen des Grundes wird zum *Transzendenzproblem.*

Ist diese Verklammerung von Wahrheit, Grund, Transzendenz eine ursprünglich einige, dann muß auch die Verkettung der entsprechenden Probleme überall da ans Licht drängen, wo die Frage nach dem »Grunde«—und sei es auch nur in der Form einer ausdrücklichen Erörterung des Satzes vom Grunde—entschlossener ergriffen wird.

Schon die aus *Leibniz* angeführte Stelle verrät die Verwandtschaft zwischen »Grund«- und Seins-

15. Vgl. a. a. O. § 69 c, S. 364 ff. und überdies S. 363 Anm.

own possibility in the ground of the essence of Dasein. To anticipate, we name this ground of [reason
for] the Ontological Difference the *transcendence* of
Dasein.

If one characterizes every *way of behaving* toward being as intentional, then *intentionality* is possible only *on the basis of transcendence.* [17] It is
neither identical with transcendence nor that which
makes transcendence possible.[15]

Until now it was enough to show, in some few but
essential steps, that the essence of truth must be
sought more primordially than the traditional characterization of truth as a property of assertions
would allow. If the essence of reasons has an inner
relationship to the essence of truth, then the *problem* of reasons can likewise be at home only where
the essence of truth derives its inner possibility,
namely, in the essence of transcendence. The question about the essence of reasons becomes the *problem of transcendence.*

If this linkage of truth, reasons, and transcendence is primordially united, then a chain of corresponding problems must also come to light wherever
the question about "reasons"—if only in the form of
an explicit discussion of the principle of sufficient
reason—is grasped firmly.

The passage cited from Leibniz itself reveals the
kinship between the problem of "reasons" and that
of Being. *Verum esse* ["being true"] means *inesse
qua idem esse* ["being present or contained in" in the
sense of "being the same as"]. But for Leibniz *verum
esse*—to be *true*—also means *to be* "in truth"—sim-

15. Cf. *ibid.,* § 69 c, pp. 364 ff., and also p. 363 n.

problem. Verum esse besagt inesse qua idem esse.
Verum esse—*Wahr*sein bedeutet aber für *Leibniz*
zugleich »in Wahrheit« *sein*—esse schlechthin.
Dann ist die Idee von Sein überhaupt ausgelegt
durch inesse qua idem esse. Was ein ens zu einem
ens macht, ist die »Identität«, die rechtverstandene
Einheit, die als einfache ursprünglich einigt und
in diesem Einigen zugleich vereinzelt. Die ursprünglich (vorgreifende) einfach vereinzelnde Eini-
gung, die das Wesen von Seiendem als solchem
ausmacht, ist aber das Wesen der monadologisch
verstandenen »Subjektivität« des subjectum (Sub-
stanzialität der Substanz). Die Leibnizische Herlei-
tung des principium rationis aus dem Wesen der
Satzwahrheit bekundet so, daß ihr eine ganz bestimmte Idee von Sein überhaupt zugrunde liegt, in
deren Licht allein jene »Deduktion« möglich wird.
Erst recht zeigt sich der Zusammenhang zwischen
»Grund« und »Sein« in der Metaphysik *Kants.* In
dessen »kritischen« Schriften möchte man freilich
gemeinhin eine ausdrückliche Behandlung des
»Satzes vom Grunde« vermissen; es sei denn, daß
man für diesen fast unbegreiflichen Mangel den
Beweis der zweiten Analogie als Ersatz gelten läßt.
Allein *Kant* hat den Satz vom Grunde sehr wohl und
an ausgezeichneter Stelle seiner Kritik der reinen
Vernunft unter dem Titel des »obersten Grundsatzes aller synthetischen Urteile« erörtert. Dieser
»Satz« legt auseinander, *was überhaupt*—im Umkreis und in der Ebene der ontologischen Fragestellung Kants—*zum Sein* von Seiendem, als dem
in der Erfahrung zugänglichen gehört. Er gibt eine
Realdefinition der transzendentalen Wahrheit, d. h.

ply *esse*. The idea of Being is then rendered by the phrase *inesse qua idem esse*. What makes an *ens* [being] an *ens* is "identity." Identity is, properly understood, the simple unity which unites primordially and, in uniting, at the same time individuates. The sort of unification that anticipates primordially and individuates simply, constitutes the essence of being as such. It is the essence of the monadologically understood "subjectivity" of the *subjectum* (substantiality of the substance). Thus Leibniz' derivation of the *principium rationis* from the essence of propositional truth is, on its own evidence, based upon a particular idea of the nature of Being. Only in the light of this idea does his "deduction" become possible. The connection between "reasons" and "Being" is first shown in Kant's metaphysics. In his "critical" works one might fail, as usual, to find an explicit treatment of the "principle of sufficient reason," unless one feels that the "Proof of the Second Analogy" meets this almost inconceivable shortcoming. Yet Kant discussed the principle quite exhaustively under the heading of the "Supreme Principle of All Synthetic Judgments" in a distinguished passage of his *Critique of Pure Reason*. [18] This second "principle" explains what, at a transcendental level, [19] i.e., within the range and on the level of Kant's ontological inquiry, belongs *to the Being* of being—"being" here understood as that which is accessible in experience. It gives a positive definition of transcendental truth, which is to say that it defines the inner possibility of transcendental truth through the unity of time, the faculty of imagina-

er bestimmt ihre innere Möglichkeit durch die Einheit von Zeit, Einbildungskraft und »Ich denke«.[16] Was Kant vom Leibnizischen Satz des zureichenden Grundes sagt, er sei »eine bemerkenswürdige Hinweisung auf Untersuchungen, die in der Metaphysik noch anzustellen wären«,[17] das gilt wiederum von seinem eigenen obersten Prinzip aller synthetischen Erkenntnis, sofern sich darin das *Problem* des Wesenszusammenhangs von Sein, Wahrheit und Grund *verbirgt*. Eine daraus erst ableitbare Frage ist dann die über das Ursprungsverhältnis von transzendentaler und formaler Logik bzw. das Recht einer solchen Unterscheidung überhaupt.

Die kurze Darstellung der Leibnizischen Ableitung des Satzes vom Grunde aus dem Wesen der Wahrheit sollte den Zusammenhang des Problems des Grundes mit der Frage nach der inneren Möglichkeit der ontologischen Wahrheit, d. h. schließlich mit der *noch* ursprünglicheren und demzufolge umgreifenden Frage nach dem Wesen der Transzendenz verdeutlichen. *Die Transzendenz* ist demnach der *Bezirk,* innerhalb dessen das Problem des Grundes sich muß antreffen lassen. Diesen Bezirk gilt es in einigen Hauptzügen vor Augen zu legen.

16. Vgl. Heidegger, Kant und das Problem der Metaphysik. 1929.
17. Vgl. *Kant,* Über eine Entdeckung, nach der alle neue Kritik der reinen Vernunft durch eine ältere entbehrlich gemacht werden soll. 1790, Schlußbetrachtung über die drei vornehmlichen Eigentümlichkeiten der Metaphysik des Herrn von Leibniz. Vgl. auch die Preisschrift über die Fortschritte der Metaphysik, I. Abteilung.

tion, and the "I think."[16] What Kant says of Leibniz' principle of sufficient reason—that it is "a remarkable foreshadowing of investigations which were yet to be undertaken in metaphysics"[17]—applies to his own supreme principle of all synthetic knowledge as well. For the *problem* of the essential connection of Being, truth, and reasons lies *concealed* in that principle. From this problem alone derives the question about the primordial relationship between transcendental and formal logic [20] or even about the validity of such a distinction altogether.

Our brief presentation of Leibniz' derivation of the principle of sufficient reason from the essence of truth has aimed at clarifying the connection of the problem of reasons with the question about the inner possibility of ontological truth and ultimately with the *still* more primordial, and thereby comprehensive, question about the essence of transcendence. *Transcendence* is, we have concluded, the *realm* within which it must be possible to confront the problem of reasons. It will be worth our while to display some of the main features of this realm.

16. Cf. Heidegger, *Kant und das Problem der Metaphysik* (1929).

17. Cf. Kant, *Über eine Entdeckung, nach der alle neue Kritik der reinen Vernunft durch eine ältere entbehrlich gemacht werden soll* (1790), *Schlußbetrachtung über die drei vornehmlichen Eigentümlichkeiten der Metaphysik des Herrn von Leibniz.* Cf. also the *Preisschrift über die Fortschritte der Metaphysik,* Part I (1791).

II / Die Transzendenz als Bezirk der Frage nach dem Wesen des Grundes

EINE TERMINOLOGISCHE Vorbemerkung soll den Gebrauch des Wortes »Transzendenz« regeln und die Bestimmung des damit gemeinten Phänomens vorbereiten. Transzendenz bedeutet Überstieg. Transzendent (transzendierend) ist, was den Überstieg vollzieht, im Übersteigen verweilt. Dieses eignet als Geschehen einem Seienden. Formal läßt sich der Überstieg als eine »Beziehung« fassen, die sich »von« etwas »zu« etwas hinzieht. Zum Überstieg gehört dann solches, *woraufzu* der Überstieg erfolgt, was unzutreffend meist das »Transzendente« genannt ist. Und schließlich wird im Überstieg je *etwas* überstiegen. Diese Momente sind einem »räumlichen« Geschehen entnommen, das der Ausdruck zunächst meint.

Die Transzendenz in der zu klärenden und auszuweisenden terminologischen Bedeutung meint solches, was dem *menschlichen Dasein* eignet, und zwar nicht als eine unter anderen mögliche, zuweilen in Vollzug gesetzte Verhaltungsweise, sondern als *vor aller Verhaltung geschehende Grundverfas-*

II / Transcendence
as the Realm of the Question
about the Essence of Reasons

A PRELIMINARY REMARK on terminology
will fix the use of the word "transcendence" and
prepare the way for a definition of the phenomenon
it signifies. Transcendence means surpassing. What
executes the action of surpassing, and remains in
the condition of surpassing, is transcendent (transcending). [21] As a happening, surpassing is proper to a being. As a condition, it can be formally
construed as a "relationship" that stretches "from"
something "to" something. To surpassing, then, belongs that *toward which* the surpassing occurs, and
which is usually but improperly called the "transcendent." And finally, *something* is always surpassed in surpassing. If we take the above to be the
main features of surpassing, it is because we con-
ceive surpassing as a kind of "spatial" happening—
which is, after all, what the expression ordinarily
means. [22]

Transcendence can be understood in a second
sense, still to be clarified and explained, namely, as
signifying what is unique to *human Dasein*—unique
not as one among other possible, and occasionally

sung dieses Seienden. Allerdings hat das menschliche Dasein als »räumlich« existierendes unter
anderen Möglichkeiten auch die zu einem räumlichen »Übersteigen« einer räumlichen Schranke
oder Kluft. Die Transzendenz jedoch ist der Überstieg, der so etwas wie Existenz überhaupt und
mithin auch ein »Sich«-bewegen-im-Raume ermöglicht.

Wählt man für das Seiende, das wir je selbst
sind und als »Dasein« verstehen, den Titel »Subjekt«, dann gilt: die Transzendenz bezeichnet das
Wesen des Subjekts, ist Grundstruktur der Subjektivität. Das Subjekt existiert nie zuvor als »Subjekt«, um dann, *falls* gar Objekte vorhanden sind,
auch zu transzendieren, sondern Subjekt*sein* heißt:
in und als Transzendenz Seiendes sein. Das Transzendenzproblem läßt sich nie so erörtern, daß eine
Entscheidung gesucht wird, ob die Transzendenz
dem Subjekt zukommen könne oder nicht, vielmehr
ist das Verständnis von Transzendenz schon die
Entscheidung darüber, ob wir überhaupt so etwas
wie »Subjektivität« im Begriff haben oder nur
gleichsam ein Rumpfsubjekt in den Ansatz bringen.

Freilich wird zunächst durch die Charakteristik
der Transzendenz als Grundstruktur der »Subjektivität« für das Eindringen in diese Verfassung
des Daseins wenig gewonnen. Im Gegenteil, weil
jetzt überhaupt der ausdrückliche oder meist unaus-
drückliche Ansatz eines Subjektbegriffes eigens
abgewehrt ist, läßt sich auch die Transzendenz
nicht mehr als »Subjekt-Objekt-Beziehung« bestimmen. Dann übersteigt aber das transzendente Dasein (ein bereits tautologischer Ausdruck) weder
eine dem Subjekt vorgelagerte und es zuvor zum

actualized, types of behavior but as a *basic constitutive feature of Dasein that happens prior to all behavior*. Of course, since human Dasein exists "spatially," it can, among other things, spatially "surpass" a spatial boundary or gap. Transcendence, however, is the surpassing that makes anything like existence and thereby movement in space possible in the first place.

If we choose the term "subject" for the being which all of us are and which we understand as Dasein, then transcendence can be said to denote the essence of the subject or the basic structure of subjectivity. The subject never first exists as "subject" and then, *in the event* objects are present at hand, goes on to transcend *as well*. Instead, *to be* a subject means to be a being in and as transcending. We can never discuss the problem of transcendence if we seek first to decide whether or not transcendence uniquely characterizes the subject. Our understanding of transcendence itself involves a decision as to whether we are in fact working with a genuine concept of "subjectivity" or are merely considering, so to speak, a "truncated subject."

Characterizing transcendence as the basic structure of subjectivity—beginning *there*—will help us little in exploring the constitution of Dasein. On the contrary, since we are now expressly forbidden to introduce a concept of subject either explicitly or inexplicitly, transcendence can no longer be defined as a "subject-object relationship." Transcendent Dasein (a tautological expression in itself) surpasses neither a "boundary" which stretches out before the

Inbleiben (Immanenz) zwingende »Schranke«, noch eine »Kluft«, die es vom Objekt trennt. Die Objekte—das vergegenständlichte Seiende—sind aber auch nicht das, *woraufzu* der Überstieg geschieht. *Was* überstiegen wird, ist gerade einzig das *Seiende selbst* und zwar jegliches Seiende, das dem Dasein unverborgen sein und werden kann, mithin *auch und gerade* das Seiende, als welches »es selbst« existiert.

Im Überstieg kommt das Dasein allererst auf solches Seiendes zu, das *es* ist, auf es *als* es »selbst«. Die Transzendenz konstituiert die Selbstheit. Aber wiederum nie zunächst nur diese, sondern der Überstieg betrifft je in eins auch Seiendes, das das Dasein »selbst« *nicht* ist; genauer: im Überstieg und durch ihn kann sich erst innerhalb des Seienden unterscheiden und entscheiden, wer und wie ein »Selbst« ist und was nicht. Sofern aber das Dasein als Selbst existiert—und nur insofern—kann es »sich« verhalten *zu* Seiendem, das aber vordem überstiegen sein muß. Obzwar inmitten des Seienden seiend und von ihm umfangen, hat das Dasein als existierendes die Natur immer schon überstiegen.

Was da nun aber jeweils in einem Dasein an Seiendem überstiegen ist, hat sich nicht einfach zusammengefunden, sondern das Seiende ist, wie immer es im Einzelnen bestimmt und gegliedert sein mag, im vorhinein in einer Ganzheit überstiegen. Diese mag dabei als solche unerkannt bleiben, wenn sie auch immer—aus jetzt nicht zu erörternden Gründen—vom Seienden her und meist aus einem eindringlichen Bezirk desselben gedeutet und daher zum mindesten gekannt ist.

subject and forces it to "remain in" (immanence) nor a "gap" which separates it from the object. Moreover, objects—objectified beings—are not that *toward which* surpassing happens. *What* is surpassed is simply *being itself,* i.e., every being which can be or become unconcealed to Dasein, *even and precisely* the very being as which Dasein "itself" exists.

In surpassing, Dasein first attains to the being that *it* is; what it attains to is its "self." Transcendence constitutes selfhood. [23] On the other hand, not only transcendence, but also surpassing, touches on a kind of being that Dasein "itself" is *not*. More accurately: only in and through surpassing can we distinguish and decide, within the realm of being, who and how a "self" is and what it is not. Only insofar as Dasein exists as a self can it relate "itself" *to* [behave *toward*] being—which in turn must be surpassed beforehand. Although Dasein *is* in the midst of, and surrounded by, being, it has always, as existing, already surpassed nature.

The being that Dasein surpasses is not a random aggregate of objects, but, however it may be defined and articulated in any particular case, is always surpassed in a totality. In the process this totality may remain unknown, even if—for reasons we will not discuss here—it is interpreted in terms of being, or some prominent realm of being, so that we seem to have at least some acquaintance with it.

Surpassing occurs totally. It never merely occurs "sometimes and sometimes not," as might a theoretical knowing of objects. Rather, surpassing is there with the fact of Being-there [Dasein]. [24]

Der Überstieg geschieht in Ganzheit und nie nur zuweilen und zuweilen nicht, etwa gar lediglich und zuerst als theoretisches Erfassen von Objekten. Mit dem Faktum des Da-seins ist vielmehr der Überstieg da.

Wenn nun aber das Seiende *nicht* das ist, *woraufhin* der Überschritt erfolgt, wie muß dieses »Woraufhin« dann bestimmt, ja überhaupt gesucht werden? Wir nennen das, *woraufhin* das Dasein als solches transzendiert, die *Welt* und bestimmen jetzt die Transzendenz als *In-der-Welt-sein*. Welt macht die einheitliche Struktur der Transzendenz mit aus; als ihr zugehörig heißt der Weltbegriff ein *transzendentaler*. Mit diesem Terminus wird alles benannt, was wesenhaft zur Transzendenz gehört und seine innere Möglichkeit von ihr zu Lehen trägt. Und erst deshalb kann auch die Erhellung und Auslegung der Transzendenz eine »transzendentale« Erörterung genannt werden. Was allerdings »transzendental« besagt, darf nun nicht einer Philosophie entnommen werden, der man das »Transzendentale« als »Standpunkt« und gar »erkenntnistheoretischen« zuweist. Das schließt die Feststellung nicht aus, daß gerade *Kant* das »Transzendentale« als Problem der inneren Möglichkeit von Ontologie überhaupt erkannt hat, obzwar für ihn das »Transzendentale« noch eine wesentlich »kritische« Bedeutung behält. Das Transzendentale betrifft für *Kant* die »Möglichkeit« (das Ermöglichende) derjenigen Erkenntnis, die *nicht zu Unrecht* die Erfahrung »überfliegt«, d. h. nicht »transzendent«, sondern Erfahrung selbst ist. Das Transzendentale gibt so die obzwar einschränkende, hierdurch jedoch zugleich positive Wesensbegrenzung (Definition)

However, if being is *not* that *toward which* surpassing occurs, how then must this "toward which" be defined or even investigated? That *toward which* Dasein transcends, we call the *world,* and we can now define transcendence as *Being-in-the-world.* World goes to make up the unified structure of transcendence; the concept of world is called *transcendental* because it is part of this structure. We use the term "transcendental" to designate everything that belongs by its essence to transcendence, everything that owes its inner possibility to transcendence. It is for this reason alone that we can also call the clarification and explanation of transcendence a "transcendental" discussion. A philosophy which treats the "transcendental" as a "standpoint," even as an "epistemological" standpoint, cannot give us any clue to what "transcendental" means. [25] This is not to deny that Kant, in particular, recognized the "transcendental" as a problem of the inner possibility of ontology, although for him the term also has another, essentially "critical," meaning. For Kant, the transcendental has to do with the "possibility" of (in the sense of that which makes possible) the kind of knowledge which does *not illegitimately* "go beyond" experience, i.e., which is not "transcendent" but is experience itself. Thus the transcendental furnishes a restrictive, yet thereby positive, delimitation (definition) of the essence of nontranscendent knowledge, i.e., of the ontical knowledge accessible to man. If the essence of transcendence is construed more radically and universally, it is then necessary to work out the idea of ontology, and so of metaphysics, more primordially.

der nichttranszendenten, d. i. dem Menschen als solchem möglichen ontischen Erkenntnis. Mit einer radikaleren und universaleren Fassung des Wesens der Transzendenz geht dann aber notwendig eine ursprünglichere Ausarbeitung der Idee der Ontologie und damit der Metaphysik zusammen.

Der die Transzendenz kennzeichnende Ausdruck »In-der-Welt-sein« nennt einen »Sachverhalt« und zwar einen vermeintlich leicht einsichtigen. Was jedoch damit gemeint ist, hängt davon ab, ob der Begriff *Welt* in einer vorphilosophisch vulgären oder in transzendentaler Bedeutung genommen wird. Die Erörterung einer zwiefachen Bedeutung der Rede vom In-der-Welt-sein kann das verdeutlichen.

Transzendenz, als In-der-Welt-sein gefaßt, soll dem menschlichen Dasein zukommen. Das ist aber schließlich das Trivialste und Leerste, was sich aussagen läßt: das Dasein kommt unter dem anderen Seienden auch vor und ist daher als solches antreffbar. Transzendenz bedeutet dann: unter das übrige schon Vorhandene, bzw. unter das ständig ins Unübersehliche vermehrbare Seiende gehörig. Welt ist dann der Titel für alles, was ist, die Allheit, als die das »Alles« über eine Zusammennehmung hinaus nicht weiter bestimmende Einheit. Legt man in der Rede vom In-der-Welt-sein diesen Weltbegriff zugrunde, dann muß freilich die »Transzendenz« *jedem* Seienden *als Vorhandenem* zugesprochen werden. Vorhandenes, d. i. unter anderem Vorkommendes, »*ist in der Welt*«. Besagt »transzendent« nichts weiter als »zum übrigen Seienden gehörig«, dann ist es evident unmöglich, die Transzendenz als *auszeichnende* Wesensverfassung dem mensch-

"Being-in-the-world," the expression that characterizes transcendence, denotes a "state of affairs," presumably one which can be discerned with ease. However, what this expression *means* depends on whether the concept "world" is understood in its prephilosophical, ordinary sense or in a transcendental sense. We can clarify all this by discussing the two senses in which the term "Being-in-the-world" can be used.

Transcendence, construed as Being-in-the-world, has been said to be proper to human Dasein. Yet ultimately this is the most trivial and empty thing we can say; it simply means that Dasein is found amidst other beings and so can be met with there. Transcendence, on this reading, would amount to belonging amidst the rest of what is already present at hand, amidst the sort of being that can be multiplied *ad infinitum.* "World" would denote "all that is," i.e., the entirety of being as the unity which merely *embraces,* but no further defines, "the entire sum of what is." If talk of Being-in-the-world were based on this concept of world, transcendence would have to be ascribed to *every* being qua *something present at hand.* [26] What is present at hand, i.e., what is found among other things of the same kind, would be *"in the world."* Thus, if "transcendent" means no more than "belonging to the rest of being," it is then obviously impossible to ascribe transcendence to human Dasein as the *distinctive* feature of its essential constitution. The proposition "Being-in-the-world belongs to the essence of human Dasein" would be false, even on its face. For it is not necessary that the sort

lichen *Dasein* zuzusprechen. Der Satz: zum
Wesen des menschlichen Daseins gehört das In-der-
Welt-sein, ist dann sogar evident falsch. Denn es
ist nicht wesensnotwendig, daß dergleichen Seiendes wie menschliches Dasein faktisch existiert. Es
kann ja auch *nicht* sein.

Wenn nun aber andererseits dem Dasein mit
Recht und ausschließlich das In-der-Welt-sein zugesprochen wird und zwar als Wesensverfassung,
dann kann dieser Ausdruck nicht die vorgenannte
Bedeutung haben. Dann bedeutet aber auch Welt
etwas anderes als die Allheit des gerade vorhandenen Seienden.

Dem Dasein das In-der-Welt-sein als Grundverfassung zusprechen, heißt, etwas über sein
Wesen (seine eigenste innere Möglichkeit als Dasein) aussagen. Hierbei kann gerade *nicht darauf*
als ausweisende Instanz gesehen werden, *ob* und
welches Dasein je nun gerade faktisch existiert oder
nicht. Die Rede vom In-der-Welt-sein ist keine Feststellung des faktischen Vorkommens von Dasein,
ja überhaupt keine ontische Aussage. Sie betrifft
einen das Dasein überhaupt bestimmenden Wesens-
verhalt und hat daher den Charakter einer ontologischen These. Mithin gilt: das Dasein ist nicht
deshalb ein In-der-Welt-sein, weil und nur weil es
faktisch existiert, sondern umgekehrt, es *kann* nur
als existierendes *sein*, d. h. als Dasein, *weil* seine
Wesensverfassung im In-der-Welt-sein liegt.

Der Satz: das faktische Dasein ist in einer Welt
(kommt unter anderem Seienden vor), verrät sich
als eine nichtssagende Tautologie. Die Aussage:
zum Wesen des Daseins gehört, daß es in der Welt
ist (»neben« anderem Seienden notwendig auch

of being we call human Dasein exist factically. It can also *not* be.

If, however, "Being-in-the-world" is rightly ascribed to Dasein alone as its essential constitutive feature, this expression cannot have the meaning discussed in the preceding paragraph. "World," then, will have to mean something other than the entirety of being immediately present at hand.

To ascribe Being-in-the-world to Dasein as the basic feature of its constitution is to make a statement about its essence—about its unique inner possibility as Dasein. Now we cannot determine anything about the essence of Dasein by asking *what sort of* Dasein exists factically, or *whether* Dasein exists factically at all. Our talk of Being-in-the-world does not tell for the factical presence of Dasein in the world; ontically, it says nothing. Such talk concerns an *essential* condition of Dasein, one which defines Dasein *at an ontological level,* and therefore has the character of an ontological proposition. Dasein, then, is not Being-in-the-world because and only because it exists factically; on the contrary, it *can* only *be* as existing, i.e., as Dasein, *because* its essential constitution lies in Being-in-the-world.

The proposition "Factical Dasein is in a world (is present among other beings)" proves to be an empty tautology. The assertion "It belongs to the essence of Dasein to be in the world (and so, necessarily, to be present 'alongside' other beings)" proves false. The thesis "Being-in-the-world belongs to the essence of Dasein as such" merely contains the *problem* of transcendence.

vorkommt), erweist sich als falsch. Die These: zum
Wesen von Dasein als solchem gehört das In-der-
Welt-sein, enthält das *Problem* der Transzendenz.
Die These ist ursprünglich und einfach. Hieraus
folgt nicht die Einfachheit ihrer Enthüllung, wenngleich das In-der-Welt-sein je nur in *einem,* nach
verschiedenen Graden durchsichtigen *Entwurf* in
das vorbereitende und wieder (freilich immer relativ) begrifflich abzuschließende Verständnis gebracht werden kann.

Die Transzendenz des Daseins ist mit der bishe-
rigen Charakteristik des In-der-Welt-seins nur erst
aus der Abwehr bestimmt. Zur Transzendenz gehört
Welt als das, woraufhin der Überstieg geschieht.
Das positive Problem, als was Welt verstanden, wie
der »Bezug« des Daseins zur Welt bestimmt, d. h.
wie das In-der-Welt-sein als ursprünglich einige
Daseinsverfassung begriffen werden soll, erörtern
wir hier nur in der Richtung und in den Grenzen,
die durch das leitende Problem des Grundes gefordert sind. In Absicht hierauf sei eine Interpretation des *Weltphänomens* versucht, die der Erhellung
der Transzendenz als solcher dienen soll.

Zur Orientierung über dieses transzendentale
Phänomen der Welt sei eine freilich notwendig
lückenhafte Charakteristik der Hauptbedeutungen
vorausgeschickt, die in der Geschichte des Weltbegriffes sich vordrängen. Bei solchen elementaren
Begriffen ist meist die vulgäre Bedeutung nicht die
ursprüngliche und wesentliche. Diese wird immer
wieder verdeckt und kommt nur schwer und selten
zu ihrem Begriff.

The thesis is primordial and simple. But this does not mean that it is simple to show what it means. It is not simple to show what it means even though Being-in-the-world can—with only *one project,* transparent in various degrees—be made accessible to the sort of preparatory understanding that must constantly be further developed at a conceptual level.

The transcendence of Dasein is only negatively defined in the foregoing characterization of Being-in-the-world. As that toward which surpassing takes place, world also belongs to transcendence. The positive problem—what world should be understood to mean and how the "relationship" of Dasein to the world should be defined, i.e., how Being-in-the-world as the primordially unified constitution of Dasein should be expressed conceptually—we will discuss only within the context and limits called for by the problem that has been our chief concern, the problem of reasons. To this end we will venture an interpretation of the *phenomenon of world* that ought to help elucidate transcendence.

To orient ourselves with respect to the transcendental phenomenon of world, we will first characterize, in a necessarily fragmentary manner, several fundamental meanings of the concept of world that have figured prominently in its history. Where elementary concepts like "world" are concerned, the popular is usually not the primordial and essential meaning. The latter is constantly hidden; it is only seldom expressed conceptually, and then with difficulty.

Schon in den entscheidenden Anfängen der antiken Philosophie zeigt sich etwas Wesentliches.[18] Κόσμος meint nicht dieses und jenes andrängende und bedrängende Seiende selbst, auch nicht dieses alles zusammengenommen, sondern bedeutet »Zustand«, d. h. das *Wie*, in dem das Seiende und zwar *im Ganzen* ist. Κόσμος οὗτος bezeichnet daher nicht diesen Bezirk von Seiendem in Abgrenzung gegen einen anderen, sondern diese Welt des Seienden im Unterschied von einer anderen Welt *desselben* Seienden, das ἐόν selbst κατὰ κόσμον.[19] Die Welt liegt als dieses »Wie im Ganzen« jeder möglichen Zerstückung des Seienden schon zugrunde; diese vernichtet nicht die Welt, sondern *bedarf* ihrer immer. Was ἐν τῷ ἑνὶ κόσμῳ[20] ist, hat diesen nicht erst in der Zusammenschiebung gebildet, sondern ist durch die Welt durch- und vorgängig beherrscht. Einen weiteren Wesenszug des κόσμος erkennt *Heraklit*:[21] ὁ Ἡράκλειτός φησι τοῖς ἐγρηγορόσιν ἕνα καὶ κοινὸν κόσμον εἶναι, τῶν δὲ κοιμωμένων ἕκαστον εἰς ἴδιον ἀποστρέφεσθαι. Den Wachen gehört eine und daher gemeinsame Welt, jeder Schlafende dagegen wendet sich seiner eigenen Welt zu. Hier ist die Welt in Beziehung gebracht zu Grundweisen, in denen das menschliche Dasein faktisch existiert. Im Wachen zeigt sich das Seiende in einem durchgängig einstimmigen, durchschnittlich jedermann zugänglichen Wie. Im Schlaf ist die Welt des Seienden eine ausschließlich auf das jeweilige Dasein vereinzelte.

18. Vgl. *K. Reinhardt*, Parmenides und die Geschichte der griechischen Philosophie. 1916. S. 174 f. u. 216 Anm.

19. Vgl. *Diels*, Fragmente der Vorsokratiker: *Melissos*, Fragm. 7; *Parmenides*, Fragm. 2.

20. A. a. O. *Anaxagoras*, Fragm. 8.

21. A. a. O. *Heraklit*, Fragm. 89.

The decisive origins of ancient philosophy reveal something essential to the concept of world.[18] *Kosmos* does not mean any particular being that might come to our attention, nor the sum of all beings; instead, it means something like "condition" or "state of affairs," i.e., the *How* in which being is *in its totality*. Thus, *kosmos houtos* does not designate one realm of being to the exclusion of another but rather one world of being in contrast to a different world of the same being, *eon* (being) itself *kata kosmon* (in relation to the cosmos).[19] The world as this "How in its totality" underlies every possible way of segmenting being; segmenting being does not destroy the world but *requires* it. What is *en tōi heni kosmōi* (in the one cosmos) [20] has not somehow been "combined" to form the *kosmos* but is, from the start, wholly dictated by the world (*kosmos*). Heraclitus takes note of another essential feature of the *kosmos:* [21] "The wakeful have one single cosmos that is common to all, while in sleep each man turns away from this world into his own." Heraclitus understands the world in terms of the basic ways in which human Dasein exists factically. In waking life, being shows itself in a completely harmonious way and is normally accessible to everyone. In sleep, however, the world of being is one that is restricted solely to each particular Dasein.

18. Cf. K. Reinhardt, *Parmenides und die Geschichte der griechischen Philosophie* (1916), pp. 174 f. and p. 216 n.
19. Cf. H. Diels, *Fragmente der Vorsokratiker* (1903): Melissus, Fragment 7; Parmenides, Fragment 2.
20. *Ibid.*, Anaxagoras, Fragment 8.
21. *Ibid.*, Heraclitus, Fragment 89.

Aus diesen knappen Hinweisen wird schon ein Mehrfaches sichtbar: 1. Welt meint eher ein *Wie des Seins* des Seienden als dieses selbst. 2. Dieses Wie bestimmt das Seiende *im Ganzen*. Es ist im Grunde die Möglichkeit jedes Wie überhaupt als Grenze und Maß. 3. Dieses Wie im Ganzen ist in gewisser Weise *vorgängig*. 4. Dieses vorgängige Wie im Ganzen ist selbst *relativ auf* das menschliche *Dasein*. Die Welt gehört mithin gerade dem menschlichen Dasein zu, obzwar sie alles Seiende, auch das Dasein mit in Ganzheit umgreift.

So gewiß sich dies allerdings noch wenig ausdrückliche und mehr aufdämmernde Verständnis des κόσμος in die genannten Bedeutungen zusammendrängen läßt, so unbestreitbar nennt doch das Wort oft nur das in solchem Wie erfahrene Seiende selbst.

Es ist aber kein Zufall, daß im Zusammenhang mit dem neuen ontischen Existenzverständnis, das im Christentum durchbrach, die Beziehung von κόσμος und menschlichem Dasein und damit der Weltbegriff überhaupt sich verschärfte und verdeutlichte. Die Beziehung wird so ursprünglich erfahren, daß κόσμος nunmehr direkt als Titel für eine bestimmte Grundart menschlicher Existenz in Gebrauch kommt. Κόσμος οὗτος bedeutet bei Paulus (vgl. 1. Kor. u. Gal.) nicht nur und nicht primär den Zustand des »Kosmischen«, sondern den Zustand und die Lage des *Menschen,* die Art seiner Stellung *zum* Kosmos, seiner Schätzung der Güter. Κόσμος ist das Menschsein im Wie einer gottabgekehrten Gesinnung (ἡ σοφία τοῦ κόσμου). Κόσμος οὗτος meint das menschliche Dasein in einer bestimmten »geschicht-

These brief remarks have already called several things to our attention: 1. World means a *How of the Being* of being rather than being itself. 2. This How defines being *in its totality*. It is ultimately the possibility of every How as limit and measure. 3. This How in its totality is in a certain way *primary*. 4. This primary How in its totality is itself *relative to* human *Dasein*. Thus the world belongs strictly to human Dasein, although it encompasses all being, Dasein included, in its totality.

This understanding of *kosmos,* while still not very explicit, is gradually becoming clearer and can be expressed in terms of the meanings of the word *"kosmos"* that we have discussed so far. Yet, just as indisputably, the term often refers merely to being itself as experienced in such a How.

It is no accident that in connection with the new ontical understanding of existence that appeared in Christianity the relationship of *kosmos* to human Dasein, and so even the concept of world, was focused and clarified. This relationship was at the time experienced so profoundly that *kosmos* thereafter came to signify a basic type of human existence. In Paul (cf. I Corinthians and Galatians), *kosmos houtos* means not merely, or even primarily, the condition of the "cosmic," but the condition and the situation of man, the character of his stance *with regard to* the cosmos and of his evaluations of what is good. *Kosmos* is the Being of man in the How of a way of thinking that is estranged from God (*hē sophia tou kosmou:* wisdom of the world). *Kosmos houtos* refers to human Dasein, involved in a particular "historical" existence, as opposed to an-

lichen« Existenz, unterschieden gegen eine andere schon angebrochene (αἰὼν ὁ μέλλων).

Ungewöhnlich häufig—vor allem im Verhältnis zu den Synoptikern—und zugleich in einem ganz zentralen Sinne gebraucht das *Johannesevangelium* [22] den Begriff κόσμος. Welt bezeichnet die gottentfernte Grundgestalt des menschlichen Daseins, den *Charakter des Menschseins* schlechthin. Demzufolge ist dann Welt auch ein regionaler Titel für alle Menschen zusammen ohne Unterschied zwischen Weisen und Törichten, Gerechten und Sündern, Juden und Heiden. Die zentrale Bedeutung dieses völlig anthropologischen Weltbegriffes kommt darin zum Ausdruck, daß er als Gegenbegriff zur Gottessohnschaft Jesu fungiert, die ihrerseits als Leben (ζωή), Wahrheit (ἀλήθεια), Licht (φῶς) begriffen wird.

Diese im Neuen Testament anhebende Bedeutungsprägung von κόσμος zeigt sich dann unverkennbar z. B. bei *Augustinus* und *Thomas von Aquino*. Mundus bedeutet nach *Augustinus* einmal das Ganze des Geschaffenen. Aber ebensooft steht mundus für mundi habitatores. Dieser Terminus hat wieder den spezifisch existenziellen Sinn der dilectores mundi, impii, carnales. Mundus *non* dicuntur *iusti*, quia licet carne in eo habitent, *corde* cum deo sunt.[23] *Augustinus* wird diesen Weltbegriff, der dann

22. Bezüglich der Textstellen aus dem Johannesevangelium vgl. den Exkurs über κόσμος bei W. *Bauer*, Das Johannesevangelium (Lietzmanns Handbuch zum Neuen Testament 6), 2. völlig neubearbeitete Aufl., 1925, S. 18.—Zur theologischen Interpretation die ausgezeichneten Darlegungen von A. *Schlatter*, Die Theologie des Neuen Testaments. II. Teil, 1910, S. 114 ff.

23. *Augustinus*, Opera (Migne), tom. IV, 1842.

other existence that has already begun (*aiōn ho mellōn*).

The Gospel of John uses the concept of *kosmos* with uncommon frequency—particularly in contrast with the Synoptic Gospels—and at the same time in a very central sense.[22] "World" stands for the basic form of human Dasein as estranged from God or, more simply, the *character of the Being of man.* "World" is also, then, a regional [27] term for the whole of mankind, without distinction of wise men and fools, righteous men and sinners, Jews and Gentiles. The central meaning of this wholly anthropological concept of world is expressed in its function as an opposing concept to the divine filiation of Jesus, which is itself conceived as life (*zōē*), truth (*alētheia*), and light (*phōs*).

Initiated in the New Testament, this usage of "*kosmos*" becomes unmistakable in, for example, Augustine and Thomas Aquinas. In Augustine, *mundus* sometimes means the whole of creation. But it just as often stands for *mundi habitatores,* a term which has the uniquely existentiell [28] sense of "those who delight in the world, the impious, the carnal. The *just* are *not* called the world, since, though they may dwell in the world in flesh, *in heart* they are with God." [23] This concept of world, which influenced the cultural history of the West, is something Augustine might just as well have drawn from

22. Regarding the passages from the text of the Gospel of John cf. the excursus on *kosmos* in W. Bauer, *Das Johannesevangelium* (Lietzmanns Handbuch zum Neuen Testament, No. 6, 2d rev. ed., 1925), p. 18. For a theological interpretation see the excellent exposition of A. Schlatter, *Die Theologie des Neuen Testaments* (1910), Part II, pp. 114 ff.

23. Augustine, *Opera* (ed. Migne), Vol. IV (1842).

die abendländische Geistesgeschichte mitbestimmte,
ebensosehr aus *Paulus* wie aus dem *Johannesevangelium* geschöpft haben. Dafür mag folgende Stelle
aus dem Tractatus in Joannis Evangelium einen
Beleg geben. Augustinus gibt zu Joh. (Prolog) 1, 10
ἐν τῷ κόσμῳ ἦν, καὶ ὁ κόσμος δι᾽ αὐτοῦ ἐγένετο· καὶ ὁ κόσμος αὐτὸν
οὐκ ἔγνω eine Auslegung von mundus, bei der er den
zweimaligen Gebrauch von mundus in »mundus per
ipsum factus est« und »mundus eum non cognovit«
als einen *zweifachen* nachweist. In der ersten Bedeutung besagt mundus soviel wie ens creatum. In
der zweiten meint mundus das habitare corde in
mundo als amare mundum, was sich deckt mit non
cognoscere Deum. Im Zusammenhang lautet die
Stelle:

> Quid est, *mundus factus est per ipsum*? Coelum,
> terra, mare et omnia quae in eis sunt, mundus dicitur.
> Iterum alia significatione, dilectores mundi mundus
> dicitur. *Mundus per ipsum factus est, et mundus eum
> non cognovit.* Num enim coeli non cognoverunt
> Creatorem suum, aut angeli non cognoverunt Crea-
> torem suum, aut non cognoverunt Creatorem suum
> sidera, quem confitentur daemonia? Omnia undique
> testimonia perhibuerunt. Sed qui non cognoverunt?
> Qui amando mundum dicti sunt mundus. Amando
> enim habitamus corde: amando autem, hoc appellari
> meruerunt quod ille, ubi habitabant. Quomodo dici-
> mus, mala est illa domus, aut, bona est illa domus,
> non in illa quam dicimus malam, parietes accusamus,
> aut in illa, quam dicimus bonam, parietes laudamus,
> sed malam domum: inhabitantes malos, et bonam
> domum: inhabitantes bonos. Sic et mundum, qui in-
> habitant amando mundum. Qui sunt? Qui diligunt

Paul as from the Gospel of John. The following
passage from the Prologue to the Gospel (John
1:10) may serve as proof: "He was in the world,
and the world was made by him, and the world
knew him not." Augustine appends an exegesis to
this passage in which he points out that the term
mundus, employed *twice* in the phrases *"mundus
per ipsum factus est"* and *"mundus eum non cognovit,"* is also employed in *two* different senses. In
the first sense, *mundus* means no more than *ens
creatum.* In the second, *mundus* means *habitare
corde in mundo* [dwelling in the world in heart], as
amare mundum [loving the world], which comes to
the same thing as *non cognoscere Deum* [not knowing God]. Set in context, his exegesis runs as follows:

> What does it mean to say: "The world was made
> by Him"? Heaven and earth, sea, and all things
> which are in them are called the world. Yet in an-
> other sense, those who delight in the world are called
> the world. "The world was made by Him, and the
> world knew Him not." But did the heavens not know
> their creator, did the angels not know their creator,
> did the stars not know their creator, whom even the
> devils acknowledged? Everywhere, all things bore
> witness to Him. Who did not know Him? Those who,
> because they love the world, are called the world. For,
> when we love a place, we dwell there in heart. And, if
> we love the place where we live, we deserve to be
> called what it is called. When we say this house is
> bad or that house is good, we do not find fault with
> the walls of the house we call bad, nor do we praise
> the walls of the house we call good. Rather, what we
> mean by "bad house" is "bad inhabitants" and, by
> "good house," "good inhabitants." In the same way,

mundum, ipsi enim corde habitant in mundo. Nam
qui non diligunt mundum, carne versantur in mundo,
sed corde inhabitant coelum.[24]

Welt bedeutet demnach: Das Seiende im Ganzen und zwar als das entscheidende Wie, gemäß
dem sich menschliches Dasein zum Seienden stellt
und hält. Ebenso gebraucht *Thomas von Aquino*
mundus einmal gleichbedeutend mit universum,
universitas creaturarum, dann aber auch in der
Bedeutung von saeculum (weltliche Gesinnung),
quod mundi nomine amatores mundi significantur.
Mundanus (saecularis) ist der Gegenbegriff zu spiritualis.[25]

Ohne Eingehen auf den Weltbegriff bei *Leibniz*
sei die Bestimmung der Welt in der Schulmetaphysik erwähnt. *Baumgarten*[26] definiert: mundus
(universum, $\pi\hat{\alpha}\nu$) est series (multitudo, totum)
actualium finitorum, quae non est pars alterius.
Welt ist hier mit der Allheit des Vorhandenen und
zwar im Sinne des *ens creatum* gleichgesetzt. Das
sagt aber: die Auffassung des Weltbegriffes ist ab-
hängig vom Verständnis des Wesens und der Möglichkeit der Gottesbeweise. Das wird besonders
deutlich bei *Chr. A. Crusius*, der den Begriff einer
Welt also definiert: »eine *Welt* heißt eine solche
reale Verknüpfung endlicher Dinge, welche nicht
selbst wiederum ein Teil von einer andern ist, zu
welcher sie vermittelst einer realen Verknüpfung

24. l. c. tract. II, cap. 1, n. 11, tom. III, 1393.
25. Vgl. z. B. S. th. II², qu. CLXXXVIII, a 2, ad 3; du-
pliciter aliquis potest esse in saeculo: uno modo per prae-
sentiam corporalem, alio modo per mentis affectum.
26. Metaphysica, ed. II, 1743, § 354, p. 87.

by "world" we mean those who dwell in the world by virtue of loving the world. Who are they? Those who delight in the world, since these same dwell in the world in their hearts. For those who do not delight in the world are engaged in the world in their flesh, but in their hearts they dwell in heaven.[24]

Thus, "world" means: being in its totality as the definitive How in accordance with which human Dasein positions and holds itself with respect to being. Aquinas sometimes uses *mundus* as synonymous with *universum* [universe] or *universitas creaturarum* [the whole world of creatures], but then he also uses it in the sense of *saeculum* [worldly way of thinking]. *Mundanus (saecularis)* is the opposite of *spiritualis*.[25]

Without entering upon any detailed discussion of the concept of world in Leibniz, we should mention the definition of world in "School metaphysics." [29] Baumgarten defines the term as follows: "The world (*universum, pan*) is that series (*multitudo, totum*) of actually existing, finite things which is not equivalent to something else." [26] Here world is equated with the entirety of that which is present at hand as *ens creatum*—which means that, to grasp the concept of world, we must understand the essence and possibility of the proofs of the existence of God. This becomes particularly clear in the work of Christian A. Crusius, who defines the concept of a world thus: ". . . a world is a real connection of

24. *Ibid.*, Tract. II, cap. 1, n. 11, Vol. III, 1393.
25. Cf., e.g., *Summa theologica*, II/2, qu. CLXXXVIII, a 2, ad 3: "Someone can be in the secular world in two senses: in one sense, by virtue of his corporeal presence; in another sense, by virtue of his state of mind."
26. *Metaphysica* (2d ed.; 1743), § 354, p. 87.

gehörte«.[27] Der Welt wird demnach entgegengesetzt Gott selbst. Sie ist aber auch unterschieden von einem »*einzelnen* Geschöpf«, nicht minder von »*mehreren zugleich seienden Geschöpfen*«, die »*in gar keiner* Verknüpfung stehen«, und schließlich ist Welt auch unterschieden von einem solchen Inbegriffe von Geschöpfen, »welcher *nur ein Teil* von einem anderen ist, mit welchem er in realer Verknüpfung stehet«.[28]

Was nun zu einer solchen Welt an wesentlichen Bestimmungen gehört, das muß sich aus einer zwiefachen Quelle ableiten lassen. In jeder Welt muß einmal vorhanden sein, »was aus dem allgemeinen Wesen der Dinge folget«. Sodann all das, was sich »bei Setzung gewisser Geschöpfe aus den wesentlichen Eigenschaften Gottes als notwendig erkennen läßt«.[29] Deshalb ist auch die »Weltlehre« im Ganzen der Metaphysik nachgeordnet der Ontologie (der Lehre von dem Wesen und den allgemeinsten Unterschieden der Dinge überhaupt) und der »theoretischen natürlichen Theologie«. Welt ist sonach der regionale Titel für die höchste Verknüpfungseinheit der Allheit des geschaffenen Seienden.

Wenn so der Weltbegriff als ein Grundbegriff der Metaphysik (der rationalen Kosmologie als einer Disziplin der Metaphysica specialis) fungiert, *Kants* Kritik der reinen Vernunft aber eine Grundlegung der Metaphysik im Ganzen darstellt,[30] dann muß hier das Problem des Weltbegriffes entsprechend

27. Entwurf der notwendigen Vernunft-Wahrheiten, wiefern sie den zufälligen entgegengesetzt werden. Leipzig 1745, § 350, S. 657.
28. A. a. O. § 349, S. 654 ff.
29. A. a. O. § 348, S. 653.
30. Vgl. darüber: Kant und das Problem der Metaphysik. 1929.

finite things which is not itself, however, a part of something else to which it might belong by virtue of a real connection." [27] Hence God Himself is set over against the world. "World" is also distinguished from any *"individual* created thing" and, no less, from *"various created things which exist at the same time"* and which "stand *in no* connection *at all."* Finally, "world" is distinguished from any aggregate of created things "that is *only a part* of something else, with which it stands in real connection." [28]

Whatever the essential characteristics of such a world, Crusius continues, they must be derivable from a twofold source. In every world, "what follows from the universal essence of things" must at some time be present at hand and so, too, all that "can be known as necessary by positing that certain created things follow from the essential properties of God." [29] Within the whole context of School metaphysics, then, even the "doctrine of world" is subordinated both to ontology (the doctrine of the essence and most universal differences of things) and to "theoretical natural theology." World is, on this view, a regional term for the supreme unity of connection of the entirety of created being.

Granted that the concept of world functions as a basic concept of metaphysics (of rational cosmology as a discipline of *metaphysica specialis*), Kant's *Critique of Pure Reason* lays the foundation for the whole of metaphysics,[30] and as a result the problem

27. *Entwurf der notwendigen Vernunft-Wahrheiten, wiefern sie den zufälligen entgegengesetzt werden* (Leipzig, 1745), § 350, p. 657.

28. *Ibid.,* § 349, pp. 654 ff.

29. *Ibid.,* § 348, p. 653.

30. Cf. Heidegger, *Kant und das Problem der Metaphysik* (1929).

der Verwandlung der Idee der Metaphysik eine
veränderte Gestalt gewinnen. Hierauf aber bedarf
es um so mehr eines freilich nur gedrängten Hin-
weises, als neben der »kosmologischen« Bedeutung
von »Welt« in Kants Anthropologie wieder die
existenzielle, freilich ohne die spezifisch christliche
Färbung, durchbricht.

Schon in der »Dissertation von 1770«, wo die
einleitende Kennzeichnung des Begriffes mundus
sich zum Teil noch ganz in der Bahn der überlieferten ontischen Metaphysik bewegt,[31] rührt *Kant* an
eine Schwierigkeit im Weltbegriff, die sich später
in der Kritik der reinen Vernunft zu einem Haupt-
problem verschärft und ausweitet. *Kant* beginnt die
Erörterung des Weltbegriffes in der »Dissertation«
mit einer formalen Bestimmung dessen, was unter
»Welt« verstanden wird: Welt ist wesenhaft als
»terminus« auf »Synthesis« bezogen: In composito
substantiali, quemadmodum Analysis non termina-
tur nisi parte quae non est totum, h. e. *Simplici,* ita
synthesis non nisi toto quod non est pars, i. e.
Mundo. In § 2 kennzeichnet er diejenigen »Momente«, die für eine Definition des Weltbegriffes
wesentlich sind: 1. *Materia* (in sensu transcenden-
tali) h. e. *partes,* quae hic sumuntur esse *substan-
tiae.* 2. *Forma,* quae consistit in substantiarum *coor-
dinatione,* non subordinatione. 3. *Universitas,* quae
est omnitudo compartium *absoluta.* Bezüglich dieses
dritten Moments bemerkt *Kant: Totalitas* haec absoluta, quanquam conceptus quotidiani et facile
obvii speciem prae se ferat, praesertim cum negative enuntiatur, sicuti fit in definitione, tamen peni-
tius perpensa crucem figere philosopho videtur.

31. De mundi sensibilis atque intelligibilis forma et principiis, Sectio I. De notione mundi generatim. §§ 1, 2.

of the concept of world must assume a different form—reflecting the transformation of the idea of metaphysics. But if the problem is to assume a different form, it all the more requires some directive which, though of course forced, can guide us toward its solution. For, in Kant's anthropology, the existentiell meaning of "world" reappears, without its peculiarly Christian nuances, alongside the "cosmological" meaning.

As early as the "Dissertation of 1770," where, to some extent, the introductory characterization of the concept *mundus* still moves along the path of traditional ontical metaphysics,[31] Kant touches on a difficulty in the concept of world that later, in the *Critique of Pure Reason,* is focused and enlarged to become a major problem. He begins his discussion of the concept of world in the "Dissertation" with a formal definition of what we should understand by the term "world." As *terminus* [limit], world is essentially related to "synthesis": "Just as, in dealing with a complex of substances, analysis only ends with a part which is not a whole, i.e., with the *simple;* so synthesis only ends with a whole which is not a part, i.e., with the *world.*" In § 2 he characterizes those "factors" which are essential to a definition of the concept of world: "1. *Matter* (in a transcendental sense), i.e., the *parts* [of a world] which are here assumed to be *substances.* 2. *Form,* which consists in the *coordination,* not in the subordination, of substances. 3. *Entirety,* which is the absolute totality of conjoined parts." Apropos of the third factor, Kant remarks: "This absolute totality appears to be

31. *De mundi sensibilis atque intelligibilis forma et principiis,* § I; "De notione mundi generatim," §§ 1, 2, in *Werke* (Cassirer ed., 1912), Vol. II.

Dieses »Kreuz« lastete im nächsten Jahrzehnt
auf Kant; denn in der Kritik der reinen Vernunft
wird gerade diese »universitas mundi« zum Problem
und zwar in mehrfacher Hinsicht. Es gilt zu klären:
1. *Worauf* bezieht sich die unter dem Titel »Welt«
vorgestellte Totalität, bzw. worauf kann sie sich
allein beziehen? 2. *Was* ist demgemäß im Weltbegriff vorgestellt? 3. Welchen *Charakter* hat dieses
Vorstellen von solcher Totalität, d. h. welches ist
die Begriffsstruktur des Welt*begriffs* als solchen?
Kants Antworten auf diese von ihm selbst so nicht
ausdrücklich gestellten Fragen bringen eine völlige
Veränderung des Weltproblems. Zwar bleibt auch
für Kants Weltbegriff erhalten, daß die in ihm
vorgestellte Totalität sich auf die *endlichen* vorhandenen Dinge bezieht. Allein dieser für den Gehalt
des Weltbegriffs wesentliche Bezug auf Endlichkeit
erhält einen neuen Sinn. Die Endlichkeit der vorhandenen Dinge wird nicht bestimmt auf dem
Wege einer ontischen Nachweisung ihres Geschaf-
fenseins durch Gott, sondern wird ausgelegt im Hinblick darauf, daß die Dinge und inwiefern sie möglicher Gegenstand für ein endliches Erkennen
sind, d. h. für ein solches, das sie als schon vorhandene sich allererst *geben* lassen muß. Dieses hinsichtlich seiner Zugänglichkeit auf ein empfangen-
des Hinnehmen (endliche Anschauung) angewiesene
Seiende selbst nennt *Kant* die »Erscheinungen«,
d. h. »Dinge in der Erscheinung«. *Dasselbe Seiende,*
verstanden jedoch als möglicher »Gegenstand« einer
absoluten, d. i. schöpferischen Anschauung, nennt
er die »Dinge an sich«. Die Einheit des Zusammenhangs der Erscheinungen, d. i. die Seinsverfassung
des in endlicher Erkenntnis zugänglichen Seienden

an ordinary, easily understandable concept, especially when it is negatively expressed as in our original definition. But, when more closely considered, it is seen to confront the philosopher with a crucial problem [cross]."

During the next decade this "cross" weighed heavily on Kant. In the *Critique of Pure Reason,* the *universitas mundi* becomes a problem in several respects. The following questions are worth clarifying, then: 1. *To what* is the totality represented by the term "world" related, i.e., to what can it alone be related? 2. What is then represented by the concept of world? 3. What *character* does the *representing* of such a totality have, i.e., what is the conceptual structure of the *concept* of world? Kant's own answers to these questions, which he himself does not pose in so explicit a manner, completely transformed the problem of world. It is true that the totality which he takes to be represented in his concept of world is a totality of those *finite* things which are present at hand. But this relationship to finitude —essential to the content of the concept of world— acquires a new sense. Kant does not establish the finitude of things present at hand by showing, ontically, that they have been created by God. He instead explains their finitude by pointing out that they are things only insofar as they are possible objects of finite knowledge, i.e., of a knowing that must let them *give* themselves as already present at hand in the first place. The sort of being which becomes accessible only in sensory accepting (finite intuition) Kant calls "appearances" or "things [as given] in appearance." *The same beings*, understood as the possible "object" of an absolute or creative

wird bestimmt durch die ontologischen Grundsätze,
d. h. das System der synthetischen Erkenntnisse a
priori. Der in diesen »synthetischen« Grundsätzen
a priori vorgestellte Sachgehalt, ihre »Realität« in der
alten und gerade von Kant festgehaltenen Bedeutung von Sachheit, läßt sich erfahrungsfrei anschau-
lich aus den Objekten, d. h. aus dem mit diesen notwendig a priori Angeschauten, der reinen Anschauung »Zeit« darstellen. Ihre Realität ist eine objektive, von den Objekten her darstellbare. Gleichwohl
ist die *Einheit der Erscheinungen,* weil notwendig
angewiesen auf ein faktisch zufälliges Gegeben-
werden, jederzeit *bedingt* und grundsätzlich un-
vollständig. Wird nun diese Einheit des Mannigfaltigen der Erscheinungen als vollständig vorgestellt,
dann erwächst das Vorstellen eines Inbegriffes, dessen Gehalt (Realität) sich grundsätzlich nicht in
einem Bilde, d. h. einem Anschaubaren entwerfen
läßt. Diese Vorstellung ist »transzendent«. Sofern
aber diese Vorstellung einer Vollständigkeit gleichwohl a priori notwendig ist, hat sie obzwar transzendent doch *transzendentale Realität.* Vorstellungen
dieses Charakters nennt *Kant* »Ideen«. Sie »enthalten eine gewisse Vollständigkeit, zu welcher keine
mögliche empirische Erkenntnis zulangt, und die
Vernunft hat dabei nur eine systematische Einheit
im Sinne, welcher sie die empirisch mögliche Einheit zu nähern sucht, ohne sie jemals völlig zu errei-
chen«.[32] »Ich verstehe aber unter einem Systeme die
Einheit der mannigfaltigen Erkenntnisse unter einer

32. Vgl. Kritik der reinen Vernunft, A 568, B 596.

intuition (*intuitus originarius*), he calls "things in themselves." The unity of the connection of appearances, i.e., the essential constitution of the Being of being as accessible in finite knowledge, is determined by ontological principles, i.e., the system of synthetic *a priori* knowledge. The factual content represented *a priori* in these "synthetic" principles —their "reality" in the old sense of factuality, a sense that Kant holds to—can be explained both independently of experience and intuitively, in terms of the objects of the pure intuition, "time," i.e., in terms of that which is, necessarily and *a priori,* intuited along with these objects. The synthetic principles have an objective reality, a reality that can be explained in terms of objects. Yet the *unity of appearances,* because it is necessarily dependent on a factically contingent givenness, is always *conditioned* and, in principle, incomplete. Now if we represent the unity of the manifold of appearances as complete, we can then represent an aggregate whose content (reality) cannot, in principle, be projected in an image, i.e., in something "intuitable." This representation is said to be "transcendent." But insofar as this representation of a completeness is a matter of *a priori* necessity, it has *transcendental* as well as transcendent *reality.* Representations of such a character Kant calls "ideas." They "contain a certain completeness which empirical knowledge never attains; reason uses them strictly in pursuit of a systematic unity, to which it seeks to approximate the empirically possible unity, without ever fully attaining its goal." [32] "But by a system I understand the unity of the manifold items of knowledge under an

32. Cf. *Kritik der reinen Vernunft,* A 568, B 596.

Idee. Diese ist der Vernunftbegriff von der Form eines Ganzen«.[33] Die in den Ideen vorgestellte Einheit und Ganzheit kann sich, weil sie »niemals im Bilde zu entwerfen ist«,[34] auch nie unmittelbar auf Anschauliches beziehen. Sie betrifft daher als höhere Einheit immer nur die Einheit der Synthesis des Verstandes. Diese Ideen aber »sind nicht willkürlich erdichtet, sondern durch die Natur der Vernunft selbst aufgegeben und beziehen sich daher notwendig auf den ganzen Verstandesgebrauch«.[35] Als reine Vernunftbegriffe entspringen sie nicht der immer noch auf Gegebenes bezogenen Reflexion des Verstandes, sondern dem reinen Verfahren der Vernunft als schließender. Kant nennt die Ideen daher, im Unterschied von den »reflektierten« Begriffen des Verstandes, »geschlossene« Begriffe.[36] Im Schließen aber geht die Absicht der Vernunft darauf, das Unbedingte zu den Bedingungen zu gewinnen. Die Ideen als reine Vernunftbegriffe der Totalität sind daher Vorstellungen des Unbedingten.

Also ist der transzendentale Vernunftbegriff kein anderer als der von der *Totalität der Bedingungen* zu einem gegebenen Bedingten. Da nun das *Unbedingte* allein die Totalität der Bedingungen möglich macht, und umgekehrt die Totalität der Bedingungen jederzeit selbst unbedingt ist, so kann ein reiner Vernunftbegriff überhaupt durch den Begriff des Unbedingten, sofern er einen Grund der Synthesis des Bedingten enthält, erklärt werden.[37]

33. A. a. O. A 832, B 860.
34. A. a. O. A 328, B 384.
35. A. a. O. A 327, B 384.
36. A. a. O. A 310, B 367; ferner A 333, B 390.
37. A. a. O. A 322, B 379.—Zur Einordnung der »Idee« als einer bestimmten »Vorstellungsart« in die »Stufenleiter« der Vorstellungen vgl. a. a. O. A 320, B 376 f.

idea. This idea is the concept, produced by reason, of the form of a whole." [33] The unified totality represented in the ideas can never be related in any unmediated fashion to that which is intuited, since it "can never be represented in an image." [34] Thus, as a higher unity, it has only to do with the unity of the synthesis of the understanding. Ideas, however, "are not arbitrarily devised but follow from the nature of reason itself and are thereby necessarily related to the whole employment of the understanding." [35] As pure concepts of reason, they do not arise from the reflection of the understanding, which is always related to what is given, but from the pure activity of reason in inference. Hence Kant entitles the ideas, as opposed to the "reflected" concepts of the understanding, "inferred" concepts.[36] In inference, reason seeks to win the unconditioned over to conditions. So, as pure concepts of totality, the ideas are representations of the unconditioned.

The transcendental concept of reason is, then, none other than the concept of the *totality of the conditions* of a given conditioned. Since the *unconditioned* alone makes the totality of conditions possible, and conversely, since the totality of conditions is itself unconditioned, a pure concept of reason can generally be explained through the concept of the unconditioned insofar as the latter contains a ground of the synthesis of the conditioned.[37]

33. *Ibid.,* A 832, B 860.
34. *Ibid.,* A 328, B 384.
35. *Ibid.,* A 327, B 384.
36. *Ibid.,* A 310, B 367; also, A 333, B 390.
37. *Ibid.,* A 322, B 379. For the classification of the "idea" as a particular "kind of representation" in the "stepladder" of representations cf. A 320, B 376 f.

Ideen sind als Vorstellungen der unbedingten Ganzheit eines Bereiches von Seiendem notwendige Vorstellungen. Sofern nun eine dreifache Beziehung von Vorstellungen auf etwas möglich ist, auf das Subjekt und auf das Objekt und auf dieses wieder zwiefach, in endlicher Weise (Erscheinungen) und in absoluter (Dinge an sich), erwachsen drei Klassen von Ideen, denen sich die drei Disziplinen der überlieferten Metaphysica specialis zuordnen lassen. Der Weltbegriff ist demnach diejenige Idee, in der die absolute Totalität der in endlicher Erkenntnis zugänglichen Objekte a priori vorgestellt wird. Welt besagt demnach soviel wie »Inbegriff aller Erscheinungen«,[38] oder »Inbegriff aller Gegenstände möglicher Erfahrung«.[39] »Ich nenne alle transzendentalen Ideen, sofern sie die absolute Totalität in der Synthesis der Erscheinungen betreffen, Weltbegriffe«.[40] Da sich nun aber das der endlichen Erkenntnis zugängliche Seiende ontologisch betrachten läßt sowohl hinsichtlich seines Wasseins (essentia) als auch hinsichtlich seines »Daseins« (existentia) oder in der Kantischen Formulierung dieses Unterschiedes, demgemäß er auch die Kategorien und Grundsätze der transzendentalen Analytik einteilt, »*mathematisch*« und »*dynamisch*«,[41] so

38. A. a. O. A 334, B 391.
39. Was heißt: sich im Denken orientieren? 1786. WW. (Cassirer) IV, S. 355.
40. Kritik der reinen Vernunft, A 407 f., B 434.
41. »In der Anwendung der reinen Verstandesbegriffe auf mögliche Erfahrung ist der Gebrauch ihrer Synthesis entweder *mathematisch* oder *dynamisch:* denn sie gehen teils bloß auf die *Anschauung,* teils auf das *Dasein* einer Erscheinung überhaupt.« A. a. O. A 160, B 199.—Hinsichtlich der entsprechenden Unterscheidung der »Grundsätze« sagt *Kant:* »Man wird aber wohl bemerken, daß ich hier ebensowenig die Grundsätze der Mathematik im einen Falle, als

As representations of the unconditioned totality of a realm of being, ideas are necessary representations. Since representations can be related to the subject as well as to the object—and to the latter in two ways, a finite way (as appearances) and an absolute way (as things in themselves)—three classes of ideas arise, corresponding to the three disciplines of traditional *metaphysica specialis*. The concept of world is that idea in which the absolute totality of objects accessible in finite knowledge can be represented *a priori*. "World," then, means no more than "aggregate of all appearances"[38] or "aggregate of all objects of possible experience."[39] "I entitle all transcendental ideas, insofar as they have to do with absolute totality in the synthesis of appearances, concepts of world."[40] The kind of being that is accessible to finite knowledge can, ontologically, be considered with regard to both "what it is" (its *essentia*) and "the fact that it is" (its *existentia*), or, as Kant puts this distinction in classifying the categories and principles of the Transcendental Analytic, *"mathematically"* and *"dynamically."*[41]

38. *Ibid.*, A 334, B 391.
39. *Was heißt: sich im Denken orientieren?* (1786), in *Werke* (Cassirer ed.), IV, 355.
40. *Kritik der reinen Vernunft*, A 407 f., B 434.
41. "In the application of the pure concepts of the understanding to possible experience, the employment of their synthesis is either *mathematical* or *dynamical:* for they have to do partly with *intuition* and partly with the *existence* of appearance in general" (*ibid.*, A 160, B 199). Apropos of the corresponding distinction of "principles" Kant says: "But one should note that here I am occupied just as little with the principles of mathematics, on the one hand, as with the principles of general (physical) dynamics, on the other. Instead, my sole concern is with the principles of the pure understanding in relation to inner sense (without distinction of the representations given therein). It is by

ergibt sich eine Einteilung der Weltbegriffe in mathematische und dynamische. Die mathematischen Weltbegriffe sind die Weltbegriffe »in engerer Bedeutung« im Unterschied zu den dynamischen, die er auch »transzendente Naturbegriffe« nennt.[42] Gleichwohl hält es Kant für »ganz schicklich«, diese Ideen »insgesamt« Weltbegriffe zu nennen,

> weil unter Welt der Inbegriff aller Erscheinungen verstanden wird, und unsere Ideen auch nur auf das Unbedingte unter den Erscheinungen gerichtet sind, teils auch, weil das Wort Welt im transzendentalen Verstande die absolute Totalität des Inbegriffs existierender Dinge bedeutet, und wir auf die Vollständigkeit der Synthesis (wiewohl nur eigentlich im Regressus zu den Bedingungen) allein unser Augenmerk richten.[43]

In dieser Bemerkung kommt nicht nur der Zusammenhang des Kantischen Weltbegriffes mit dem der überlieferten Metaphysik an den Tag, sondern ebenso deutlich die in der Kritik der reinen Vernunft vollzogene Umwandlung, d. h. ursprünglichere ontologische Interpretation des Weltbegriffes, die sich jetzt in kurzer Beantwortung der obigen drei Fragen also kennzeichnen läßt: 1. Der Weltbegriff ist nicht

---

die Grundsätze der allgemeinen (physischen) Dynamik im anderen, sondern nur die des reinen Verstandes im Verhältnis auf den inneren Sinn (ohne Unterschied der darin gegebenen Vorstellungen) vor Augen habe, dadurch jene insgesamt ihre Möglichkeit bekommen. Ich benenne sie also mehr in Betracht der Anwendung, als um ihres Inhalts willen . . .« A. a. O. A 162, B 202.—Vgl. gerade mit Bezug auf eine radikalere Problematik des Weltbegriffs und des Seienden im Ganzen den Unterschied des Mathematisch-Erhabenen und Dynamisch-Erhabenen. Kritik der Urteilskraft, bes. § 28.

42. A. a. O. A 419 ff., B 446 ff.

43. A. a. O.

Thus, concepts of world can themselves be either mathematical or dynamical. The mathematical are concepts of world "in the narrow sense" and are opposed to the dynamical, which Kant also calls "transcendent concepts of nature." [42] Kant thinks it "quite proper" to entitle these ideas "one and all" concepts of world,

> because by world we understand the aggregate of all appearances, because our ideas are directed solely to the unconditioned in appearances, partly because in its transcendental sense the word "world" means the absolute totality of the aggregate of existing things, and finally because we direct our attention solely to the completeness of the synthesis (although actually only in the regress to conditions).[43]

This remark brings to light, not only the connection of the Kantian concept of world with that of traditional metaphysics, but also the transformation, i.e., the more original ontological interpretation, of the concept of world that Kant achieved in the *Critique of Pure Reason*. We can now sketch out the main features of that transformation and, in the process, answer the three questions we posed above: 1. The concept of world is not an ontical linkage of things in themselves but a transcendental (ontologi-

---

virtue of these principles of the pure understanding that those of mathematics and dynamics are possible. I name them, then, more with regard to their application than on account of their content . . ." (*ibid.*, A 162, B 202). For a more radical problematic of the concept of world and being in its totality cf. the distinction of the "mathematically sublime" and the "dynamically sublime" in the *Kritik der Urteilskraft* (1790), in *Werke* (Cassirer ed.), Vol. V, esp. § 28.

42. *Kritik der reinen Vernunft*, A 419 ff., B 446 ff.
43. *Ibid.*

eine ontische Verknüpfung der Dinge an sich, sondern ein transzendentaler (ontologischer) Inbegriff
der Dinge als Erscheinungen. 2. Im Weltbegriff ist
nicht dargestellt eine »Koordination« der Substan-
zen, sondern gerade eine Subordination und zwar
die zum Unbedingten »aufsteigende Reihe« der Bedingungen der Synthesis. 3. Der Weltbegriff ist
nicht eine in ihrer Begrifflichkeit unbestimmte »ra-
tionale« Vorstellung, sondern als Idee, d. i. als reiner
synthetischer Vernunftbegriff bestimmt und von
Verstandesbegriffen unterschieden.

Und so wird dem Begriff mundus nun auch der
früher zugewiesene Charakter der universitas (Allheit) genommen und einer noch höheren Klasse
transzendentaler Ideen vorbehalten, worauf der
Weltbegriff selbst eine Hinweisung enthält und die
Kant das »transzendentale Ideal« nennt.[44]

An dieser Stelle muß auf eine Interpretation
dieses höchsten Punktes der Kantischen spekulati-
ven Metaphysik verzichtet werden. Nur eines bedarf
der Erwähnung, um den Wesenscharakter des Weltbegriffs, die Endlichkeit, noch deutlicher hervortre-
ten zu lassen.

Als Idee ist der Weltbegriff die Vorstellung einer
unbedingten Totalität. Gleichwohl stellt er nicht das
schlechthin und »eigentlich« Unbedingte vor, sofern
die in ihm gedachte Totalität auf Erscheinungen,
den möglichen Gegenstand *endlicher* Erkenntnis,
bezogen bleibt. Welt als Idee ist zwar transzendent,
sie *übersteigt* die Erscheinungen, so zwar, daß sie
als *deren* Totalität gerade auf sie *zurückbezogen* ist.
Transzendenz im Kantischen Sinne des Übersteigens
der Erfahrung ist aber doppeldeutig. Sie kann ein-

44. A. a. O. A 572, B 600 Anm.

cal) aggregate of things as appearances. 2. What is exhibited in the concept of world is not a "coordination" of substances but a "subordination," namely, the "series" of the conditions of synthesis "ascending" to the unconditioned. 3. The concept of world is not to be defined as a conceptually indeterminate, "rational" representation, but as an idea, or pure synthetic concept of reason; it must therefore be distinguished from concepts of the understanding.

Thus, even the character of *universitas* (entirety), earlier attributed to the concept *mundus*, Kant now reserves for a still higher class of transcendental ideas, which the concept of world itself suggests and which Kant entitles "transcendental ideals." [44]

We must waive any interpretation of this, the highest plateau of Kantian speculative metaphysics. We need only mention one further thing in order to clarify the essential character of the concept of world: finitude.

As an idea, the concept of world is the representation of an *unconditioned* totality. Yet it does not represent the simply and "genuinely" unconditioned, since the totality thought in it remains related to appearances, the sole possible object of *finite* knowledge. World as idea is transcendent; it *surpasses* appearances in such a way that, as *their* totality, it is directly *related back* to them. Transcendence, in the Kantian sense of the surpassing of experience, has two meanings. On the one hand, it can signify: to overstep that which is given *within* experience, namely, the manifold of appearances. This holds for

44. *Ibid.,* A 572, B 600, note.

mal besagen: *innerhalb* der Erfahrung das *in ihr*
Gegebene als solches, die Mannigfaltigkeit der Erscheinungen, überschreiten. Das gilt von der Vorstellung »Welt«. Dann aber heißt Transzendenz:
aus der Erscheinung als endlicher Erkenntnis überhaupt heraustreten und das mögliche Ganze aller
Dinge als »Gegenstand« des intuitus originarius vorstellen. In dieser Transzendenz erwächst das transzendentale Ideal, demgegenüber Welt eine *Ein-
schränkung* darstellt und zum Titel der endlichen,
menschlichen Erkenntnis in ihrer Totalität wird.
Der Weltbegriff steht gleichsam *zwischen* der »Möglichkeit der Erfahrung« und dem »transzendentalen Ideal« und bedeutet so im Kern die Totalität
der Endlichkeit *menschlichen* Wesens.

Von hier aus eröffnet sich der Einblick in die
mögliche zweite, spezifisch existenzielle Bedeutung,
die bei *Kant* dem Weltbegriff neben der »kosmologischen« zukommt.

»Der wichtigste Gegenstand in der Welt, auf
den der Mensch alle Fortschritte in der Kultur an-
wenden kann, ist der *Mensch,* weil er sein eigener
letzter Zweck ist.—Ihn also seiner Spezies nach als
mit Vernunft begabtes Erdwesen zu erkennen, ver-
dient besonders *Weltkenntnis* genannt zu werden,
ob er gleich nur einen Teil der Erdgeschöpfe ausmacht«.[45] Kenntnis des *Menschen* und zwar gerade
im Hinblick »auf das, was *er* als freihandelndes Wesen aus sich selber macht oder machen kann und
soll«, also *gerade nicht* die Kenntnis des Menschen

45. Anthropologie in pragmatischer Hinsicht abgefaßt.
1800, 2. Aufl., Vorrede. WW. (Cassirer) VIII, S. 3.

the representation "world." But transcendence can also mean: to step *out of* appearance considered as finite knowledge in general and represent the possible entirety of all things as the "object" of an *intuitus originarius*. The transcendental ideal arises in this, the latter kind of transcendence; over against the ideal, world constitutes a *limit* and denotes finite, *human* knowledge in its totality. The concept of world stands, as it were, *between* the "possibility of experience" and the "transcendental ideal." Thus the concept ultimately signifies the totality of the finitude of the *human* essence [creature].

Working from here, we can win some insight into the second possible, peculiarly existentiell meaning which, in addition to its "cosmological" meaning, belongs to the Kantian concept of world.

> The most important object in the world, the object to which we can ascribe all cultural progress, is *man,* since he is his own ultimate end. Knowing him in accordance with his species, i.e., as a creature endowed with reason, should be called *knowledge about the world,* even though he makes up only part of terrestrial creation.[45] [30]

Knowledge about *man,* particularly with regard "to that which *he,* as a free agent, makes or can and ought to make of himself" (*precisely not,* then, knowledge about man considered "physiologically"), Kant calls knowledge about the *world.* Knowledge about the world is synonymous with pragmatic *anthropology* (the science of man).

---

45. *Anthropologie in pragmatischer Hinsicht abgefaßt* (2d ed., 1800), Preface, in *Werke* (Cassirer ed.), VIII, 3.

in »physiologischer« Hinsicht, wird hier Kenntnis
der *Welt* genannt. Weltkenntnis ist gleichbedeutend
mit pragmatischer *Anthropologie* (Menschen-
kunde). »Eine solche Anthropologie, als *Weltkenntnis* . . . betrachtet, wird eigentlich alsdann noch
nicht *pragmatische* genannt, wenn sie ein ausge-
breitetes Erkenntis der *Sachen* in der Welt, z. B.
der Tiere, Pflanzen und Mineralien in verschiedenen
Ländern und Klimaten, sondern wenn sie Erkenntnis des Menschen als *Weltbürgers* enthält.«[46]

Daß »Welt« gerade die Existenz des Menschen
im geschichtlichen Miteinander bedeutet und nicht
sein kosmisches Vorkommen als Spezies von Lebe-
wesen, wird noch besonders klar aus den Redewen-
dungen, die *Kant* zur Klärung dieses existenziellen
Weltbegriffes beibringt: »Welt kennen« und »Welt
haben«. Beide Ausdrücke meinen, obzwar sie beide
auf die Existenz des Menschen zielen, noch Ver-
schiedenes, »indem der eine (der die Welt kennt)
nur das Spiel *versteht,* dem er zugesehen hat, der
andere aber *mitgespielt* hat«.[47] Welt ist hier der Titel
für das »Spiel« des alltäglichen Daseins, für dieses
selbst.

---

46. A. a. O. S. 4.
47. A. a. O. »Ein Mann von Welt ist Mitspieler im großen
Spiel des Lebens.«—»*Weltmann* heißt die Verhältnisse zu
anderen Menschen und wie's im menschlichen Leben zugeht,
wissen.« »*Welt haben,* heißt Maximen haben und große Mu-
ster nachahmen. Es kommt aus dem Französischen. Zum
Zweck gelangt man durch Conduite, Sitten, Umgang usw.«
Vorlesung über Anthropologie. Vgl. Die philosophischen
Hauptvorlesungen I. Kants. Nach den neuaufgefundenen
Kolleghelten des Grafen Heinrich zu Dohna-Wundlacken.
Herausgegeben von A. Kowalewski, 1924, S. 71.

> Such an anthropology, understood as *knowledge about the world,* is not called *pragmatic* merely if it contains an extensive knowledge of *things* in the world, e.g., of animals, plants, and minerals in various countries and climates, but only if it also contains knowledge of man *as citizen of the world.*[46]

That Kant takes "world" to signify the existence of man within his historical community and not his presence in the cosmos as a species of living creature becomes especially clear if we consider the idioms he uses to clarify this existentiell concept of world: "to know [the ways of] the world" and "to have class [world]." Though both expressions refer to the existence of man, each means something different, "since the first (the person who knows the ways of the world) only *understands* the game which he witnesses, while the second has *played along* with it." [47] Here, "world" is the name for the "game" of everyday Dasein, indeed for Dasein itself.

Kant goes on to distinguish "worldly wisdom" and "personal wisdom." "The former is a man's ability to influence others in order to use them for his

46. *Ibid.,* p. 4.
47. *Ibid.* "A man of good breeding [of world] is one who plays along in the grand game of life." "To be a *man of the world* means to know how one stands with other men and how things go in life." "*To have class* [world] means to have principles and to emulate great examples. The expression comes from the French. One arrives at one's ends by means of manners, customs, dealings, etc." ("Vorlesung über Anthropologie," in *Die philosophischen Hauptvorlesungen I. Kants. Nach den neuaufgefundenen Kollegheften des Grafen Heinrich zu Dohna-Wundlacken,* edited by A. Kowalewski [1924], p. 71).

Dementsprechend unterscheidet *Kant* die »Weltklugheit« von der »Privatklugheit«. »Die erste ist die Geschicklichkeit eines Menschen, auf andere Einfluß zu haben, um sie zu seinen Absichten zu gebrauchen«.[48] Ferner: »Pragmatisch ist eine Geschichte abgefaßt, wenn sie *klug* macht, d. i. die Welt belehrt, wie sie ihren Vorteil besser oder wenigstens ebensogut als die Vorwelt besorgen könne«.[49]

Von dieser »Weltkenntnis« im Sinne der »Lebenserfahrung« und des Existenzverständnisses unterscheidet *Kant* das »Schulwissen«.[50] Am Leitfaden dieses Unterschiedes entwickelt er dann den Begriff der Philosophie nach dem »Schulbegriff« und nach dem »Weltbegriff«.[51] Philosophie im scholastischen Sinne bleibt Sache des bloßen »Vernunftkünstlers«. Philosophie nach dem Weltbegriff ist das Anliegen des »Lehrers im Ideal«, d. h. dessen, der abzielt auf den »göttlichen Menschen in uns«.[52] »Weltbegriff heißt hier derjenige, der das betrifft, was jedermann notwendig interessiert«.[53]

Welt ist in all dem die Bezeichnung für das menschliche Dasein im Kern seines Wesens. Dieser Weltbegriff entspricht vollkommen dem existenziellen des *Augustinus,* nur daß die spezifisch christliche Wertung des »weltlichen« Daseins, der amatores mundi, weggefallen ist und Welt positiv die »Mitspieler« im Spiel des Lebens bedeutet.

48. Vgl. Grundlegung zur Metaphysik der Sitten. WW. (Cassirer) IV, S. 273 Anmerkung.
49. A. a. O. S. 274 Anm.
50. Vgl. die angeführte Anthropologievorlesung S. 72.
51. Kritik der reinen Vernunft, A 839, B 867 f.—Vgl. auch *Logik* (hrsg. von G. B. Jäsche), Einleitung, Abschn. III.
52. A. a. O. A 569, B 597.
53. A. a. O. A 840, B 868 Anm.

own ends." [48] Furthermore: "A history is composed pragmatically if it makes us *wise*, i.e., teaches the world how it can secure its own advantage better than, or at least as well as, the world of former times." [49]

Kant also distinguishes "school wisdom" from this "knowledge about the world" in the sense of "experience in life." [50] Guided by this distinction, he proceeds to develop the concept of philosophy in accordance with both the "school concept" and the "concept of world." [51] Philosophy in the scholastic sense remains a subject for the mere "artificer of reason." Philosophy in accordance with the concept of world is the concern of the "ideal teacher," i.e., the teacher who aims at reaching the "divine man in us." [52] "Here, the concept of world is that concept which concerns what is necessarily of interest to everyone." [53]

Throughout the foregoing, "world" serves as the name of the essence of human Dasein. This concept of world corresponds perfectly to Augustine's existentiell concept; only the uniquely Christian evaluation of "worldly" Dasein, of the *amatores mundi,* has dropped away. "World" now assumes the positive meaning of "fellow players" in the game of life.

The *existentiell* meaning of the concept of world that we found in Kant prefigures the more recent

48. Cf. *Grundlegung zur Metaphysik der Sitten* (1785), in *Werke* (Cassirer ed.), IV, p. 273, note.

49. *Ibid.,* p. 274, note.

50. Cf. the "Vorlesung über Anthropologie," p. 72.

51. *Kritik der reinen Vernunft,* A 839, B 867, note. Cf. also Kant's *Logik,* edited by G. B. Jäsche (1800), Introduction, Section III.

52. *Kritik der reinen Vernunft,* A 569, B 597.

53. *Ibid.,* A 840, B 868, note.

Die zuletzt aus *Kant* angeführte *existenzielle*
Bedeutung des Weltbegriffes bekundet sodann der
in der Folgezeit aufkommende Ausdruck »*Weltanschauung*«.[54] Aber auch Prägungen wie »Mann von
Welt«, »vornehme Welt« zeigen eine ähnliche Bedeutung des Weltbegriffes. »Welt« ist auch hier nicht ein
bloßer regionaler Titel, der die Gemeinschaft von
Menschen bezeichnete im Unterschied von der Allheit der Naturdinge, sondern Welt meint gerade die
Menschen *in ihren Bezügen* zum Seienden im Ganzen, d. h. zur »vornehmen Welt« gehören auch z. B.
Hotels und Rennställe.

Es ist daher gleich irrig, den Ausdruck Welt entweder als Bezeichnung der Allheit der Naturdinge
(naturaler Weltbegriff) oder als Titel für die Gemeinschaft der Menschen (personaler Weltbegriff)
in Anspruch zu nehmen.[55] Vielmehr liegt das meta-

54. Die Fragen: 1. inwiefern gehört zum Wesen des
Daseins als In-der-Welt-sein notwendig so etwas wie »Weltanschauung«? 2. in welcher Weise muß im Hinblick auf
die Transzendenz des Daseins das Wesen von Weltanschauung überhaupt umgrenzt und in seiner inneren Möglichkeit
begründet werden? 3. wie verhält sich gemäß ihrem transzendentalen Charakter die Weltanschauung zur Philosophie?—können hier weder ausgearbeitet noch gar beant-
wortet werden.

55. Wenn man gar den ontischen Zusammenhang der
Gebrauchsdinge, des Zeugs, mit der Welt identifiziert und
das In-der-Welt-sein als Umgang mit den Gebrauchsdingen
auslegt, dann ist freilich ein Verständnis der Transzendenz
als In-der-Welt-sein im Sinne einer »Grundverfassung des
Daseins« aussichtslos.

Wohl hat dagegen die ontologische Struktur des »um-
weltlich« Seienden—sofern es als Zeug entdeckt ist—für
eine *erste Kennzeichnung* des Weltphänomens den Vorzug,
zur Analyse dieses Phänomens überzuleiten und das transzendentale Problem der Welt vorzubereiten. Das ist denn
auch die *einzige* und in der Gliederung und Anlage der

expression "Weltanschauung." [54] Even phrases like "a man of good breeding" [*Mann von Welt*] and "the beau monde" [*vornehme Welt*] show a similar meaning for the concept of world. Here, too, "world" is not merely a regional term for the community of men as opposed to the entirety of natural things. Instead, world simply means men *in their relationships* to being in its totality; town houses and mews, for example, also belong to "the beau monde."

It is wrong, then, to use the expression "world" either as a name for the entirety of natural things (the natural concept of world) or as a title for the community of men (the personal concept of world). [55] Metaphysically essential to the meaning of

54. The following questions can neither be elaborated nor answered here: 1. To what extent does a "Weltanschauung" necessarily belong to the essence of Dasein as Being-in-the-world? 2. In what way must the essence of the Weltanschauung be defined with regard to the transcendence of Dasein and be grounded in its inner possibility? 3. How (given its transcendental character) is the Weltanschauung related to philosophy?

55. If we somehow equate the ontical system of useful things (of tools) with the world and explain Being-in-the world as traffic with useful things, we then abandon any understanding of transcendence as Being-in-the-world in the sense of a "basic constitutive feature of Dasein." On the other hand, a study of the ontological structure of "environmental" being (insofar as it is discovered as tool) has one singular advantage for a *preliminary characterization* of the phenomenon of world: it leads over to an analysis of this phenomenon and prepares the way for the transcendental problem of world. As is indicated clearly enough in the outline and arrangement of §§ 14–24 of *Sein und Zeit*, this is the *sole* intention of the analysis of environment, which itself, considered in terms of the *guiding aim* of the book, remains subordinate. There are reasons why the concept "nature" seems to be missing in the Analytic of Dasein—not only "nature" as the object of natural science but also "nature" in a more primor-

physisch Wesentliche der mehr oder minder klar abgehobenen Bedeutung von κόσμος, mundus, Welt darin, daß sie auf die Auslegung des menschlichen Daseins *in seinem Bezug zum Seienden im Ganzen* abzielt. Aus Gründen, die hier nicht zu erörtern sind, stößt aber die Ausbildung des Weltbegriffes zuerst auf *die* Bedeutung, gemäß der er das Wie des Seienden im Ganzen kennzeichnet, so zwar, daß dessen *Bezug zum* Dasein zunächst nur unbestimmt verstanden wird. Welt gehört zu einer *bezughaften,* das Dasein als solches auszeichnenden Struktur, die das In-der-Welt-sein genannt wurde. Diese Verwendung des Weltbegriffes ist—das sollten die historischen Hinweise zeigen—so wenig willkürlich, daß sie gerade versucht, ein ständig schon bekanntes, aber ontologisch nicht einheitlich gefaßtes Daseinsphänomen in die Ausdrücklichkeit und Schärfe eines *Problems* zu heben.

Das menschliche Dasein—Seiendes *inmitten* von Seiendem befindlich, *zu* Seiendem sich verhaltend —existiert dabei so, daß das Seiende immer im

---

§§ 14–24 (Sein und Zeit) deutlich genug angezeigte Absicht der Umweltanalyse, die im Ganzen und auf das *leitende Ziel* hin angesehen von untergeordneter Bedeutung bleibt.

Wenn aber in der so orientierten Analytik des Daseins die Natur scheinbar fehlt—nicht nur die Natur als Gegenstand der Naturwissenschaft, sondern auch die Natur in einem ursprünglichen Sinne (vgl. dazu S. u. Z. S. 65 unten)—, dann bestehen dafür Gründe. Der entscheidende liegt darin, daß sich Natur weder im Umkreis der Umwelt antreffen läßt, noch überhaupt primär als etwas, *wozu* wir uns *verhalten.* Natur ist ursprünglich im Dasein offenbar dadurch, daß dieses als befindlich-gestimmtes *inmitten von* Seiendem existiert. Sofern aber Befindlichkeit (Geworfenheit) zum Wesen des Daseins gehört und in der Einheit des vollen Begriffes der *Sorge* zum Ausdruck kommt, kann allein hier erst die *Basis* für das *Problem* der Natur gewonnen werden.

kosmos (*mundus,* world)—however clearly that
meaning may be defined—is that it aim at explaining human Dasein *in Dasein's relationship to being
in its totality.* For reasons that cannot be discussed
here, the concept of world first assumes the meaning of the How of being in its totality; the *relationship* of being in its totality *to* Dasein remains, for
the most part, only vaguely understood. World belongs to a structure of *relations* which marks Dasein
out as Dasein and is entitled Being-in-the-world.
This use of the concept of world, as our remarks on
its history should have shown, is not the least bit
arbitrary but simply attempts to give the phenomenon of Dasein the clarity and explicitness of a *problem.* For, though the phenomenon is familiar
enough, it has yet to be ontologically construed in
any consistent fashion.

Human Dasein, a being situated *in the midst of*
being and relating itself *to* [behaving *toward*] being,
exists in such a way that the whole of being is
always manifest, and manifest as a totality. The
totality need not, in fact must not, be conceived in
any explicit fashion; its range is variable, and the
fact that it belongs to Dasein can be concealed. We
understand its character as a totality without grasping, or "completely" investigating, the whole of manifest being in all its peculiar connections, realms,

dial sense (cf. *Sein und Zeit,* p. 65 *et infra*). The decisive
reason is that we encounter nature neither within the com-
pass of the environment nor even as something *to which*
we *relate* ourselves [*toward which* we *behave*]. Nature is
primordially manifest in Dasein because Dasein exists as
situated and disposed *in the midst of* being. But only insofar as situatedness (thrownness) belongs to the essence of
Dasein and is expressed in the unity of the full concept of
care can we attain the *basis* for the *problem* of nature.

Ganzen offenbar ist. Die Ganzheit muß dabei nicht eigens begriffen, ihre Zugehörigkeit zum Dasein kann verhüllt sein, die Weite dieses Ganzen ist veränderlich. Die Ganzheit ist verstanden, ohne daß auch das Ganze des offenbaren Seienden in seinen spezifischen Zusammenhängen, Bezirken und Schichten eigens erfaßt oder gar »vollständig« durchforscht wäre. Das je vorgreifend-umgreifende Verstehen dieser Ganzheit aber ist Überstieg zur Welt. Es gilt nun, eine konkretere Auslegung des Weltphänomens zu versuchen. Sie ergibt sich durch die Beantwortung der beiden Fragen: 1. Welches ist der Grundcharakter der gekennzeichneten Ganzheit? 2. Inwiefern ermöglicht diese Charakteristik der Welt eine Aufhellung des Wesens des Daseinsbezugs zur Welt, d. h. eine Erhellung der inneren Möglichkeit des In-der-Welt-seins (Transzendenz)?

Welt als Ganzheit »ist« kein Seiendes, sondern das, aus dem her das Dasein *sich zu bedeuten gibt,* zu welchem Seienden und wie es sich dazu verhalten *kann.* Dasein gibt »*sich*« aus »*seiner*« Welt her zu bedeuten, heißt dann: in diesem Auf-es-zukommen aus der Welt zeitigt sich das Dasein als ein *Selbst,* d. h. als ein Seiendes, das *zu sein* ihm anheimgegeben ist. Im Sein dieses Seienden *geht es um dessen Seinkönnen.* Das Dasein ist so, daß es *umwillen seiner* existiert. Wenn aber die Welt es ist, im Überstieg zu der sich allererst Selbstheit zeitigt, dann erweist sie sich als das, worumwillen Dasein existiert. Die Welt hat den Grundcharakter des Umwillen von . . . und das in dem ursprünglichen Sinne, daß sie allererst die innere Möglichkeit für jedes faktisch sich bestimmende deinetwegen, seinetwegen, deswegen usf. vorgibt. Worumwillen aber

and strata. The understanding which anticipates and encompasses this totality is what we have called "surpassing to the world." We must now attempt to interpret the phenomenon of world more concretely. We can do so by answering two questions: 1. What is the basic character of the totality we have described? 2. To what extent does our characterization of the world make it possible to elucidate the essence of the relationship of Dasein to the world, i.e., to illuminate the inner possibility of Being-in-the-world (transcendence)?

As a totality, world "is" no particular being but rather that by means of and in terms of which Dasein *gives itself to understand* [*signify*] what beings it *can* behave toward and how it *can* behave toward them. That Dasein gives "*itself*" to understand in terms of "*its*" world means, then, that in approaching being through the world, Dasein makes a *self* of itself, i.e., a being which is free *to be*. The Being of Dasein lies in its "potentiality for being." [31] Better: its Being is such that *its potentiality for being is an issue.* Dasein exists "for the sake of its. . . ." If the world is that, in surpassing to which, selfhood first arises, it is also that for the sake of which Dasein exists. The world has the basic character of the "for the sake of . . ." in the primordial sense that it ensures the inner possibility of every factical "for your sake," "for his sake," "for its sake" ["therefore"], etc. But that for the sake of which Dasein exists is itself. World belongs to selfhood; it is essentially related to Dasein.

Dasein existiert, ist es selbst. Zur Selbstheit gehört Welt; diese ist wesenhaft daseinsbezogen.

Bevor wir versuchen, dem Wesen dieses Bezugs nachzufragen und so das In-der-Welt-sein vom Unwillen als dem primären Weltcharakter her auszulegen, bedarf es der Abwehr einiger naheliegender Mißdeutungen des Gesagten.

Der Satz: *Das Dasein existiert umwillen seiner*, enthält keine egoistisch-ontische Zwecksetzung für eine blinde Eigenliebe des jeweils faktischen Menschen. Er kann daher nicht etwa durch den Hinweis darauf »widerlegt« werden, daß viele Menschen sich *für die Andern* opfern und daß überhaupt die Menschen nicht nur für sich allein, sondern in Gemeinschaft existieren. In dem genannten Satz liegt weder eine solipsistische Isolierung des Daseins, noch eine egoistische Aufsteigerung desselben. Wohl dagegen gibt er die Bedingung der Möglichkeit dafür, daß der Mensch »sich« *entweder* »egoistisch« *oder* »altruistisch« verhalten kann. Nur weil Dasein als solches durch Selbstheit bestimmt ist, kann sich ein Ichselbst zu einem Du-selbst verhalten. Selbstheit ist die Voraussetzung für die Möglichkeit der Ichheit, die immer nur im Du sich erschließt. Nie aber ist Selbstheit auf Du bezogen, sondern—weil all das erst ermöglichend—gegen das Ichsein und Dusein und erst recht etwa gegen die »Geschlechtlichkeit« neutral. Alle Wesenssätze einer ontologischen Analytik des Daseins im Menschen nehmen dieses Seiende im vorhinein in dieser Neutralität.

Wie bestimmt sich nun der Bezug des Daseins zur Welt? Da diese kein Seiendes ist und Welt zum Dasein gehören soll, kann dieser Bezug offenbar nicht gedacht werden als die Beziehung zwischen

Before we attempt to inquire after the essence of this relationship and so to interpret Being-in-the-world in terms of the "for the sake of . . . ," the primary character of world, we must dispel some misunderstandings that are likely to arise.

The proposition "Dasein exists for the sake of its . . ." is not a statement about the egoistical or ontical ends of some blind conceit of factical man. Thus it cannot be refuted by showing that many men sacrifice themselves *for others* and that men do not, in general, exist for themselves alone but in community. The proposition represents neither a solipsistic isolation nor an egoistical exaltation of Dasein. On the contrary, it states the condition of the possibility of man's behaving *either* "egoistically" *or* "altruistically." Only because Dasein is defined by selfhood can an I-self relate "itself" to a Thou-self. Selfhood is the presupposition of the possibility of being an "I," which itself is revealed only in the "Thou." Selfhood is never related to a Thou; it is neutral toward "being an I" and "being a Thou," and even more toward "sexuality," since it is what makes them all possible in the first place. [32] All essential propositions of an ontological Analytic of Dasein in man treat Dasein in its neutrality.

How do we define the relationship of Dasein to the world? Since the world is not a being but belongs to Dasein, we obviously cannot understand it as a relationship between Dasein as one kind of being and world as another. But, if we cannot, is the world not assimilated to Dasein (the subject) and, in effect, made something purely "subjective"? [33] On

dem Dasein als dem einen Seienden und der Welt als dem anderen. Wenn nicht, wird dann die Welt nicht in das Dasein (Subjekt) hineingenommen und für etwas rein »Subjektives« erklärt? Allein es gilt doch erst durch die Aufhellung der Transzendenz eine Möglichkeit zu gewinnen für die Bestimmung dessen, was »Subjekt« und »subjektiv« besagen. Am Ende muß der Weltbegriff so gefaßt werden, daß die Welt zwar subjektiv ist, aber gerade deshalb nicht als Seiendes in die Innensphäre eines »subjektiven« Subjekts fällt. Aus demselben Grunde aber ist sie auch nicht bloß objektiv, wenn dies bedeutet: unter die seienden Objekte gehörig.

Die Welt wird als die jeweilige Ganzheit des Umwillen eines Daseins durch dieses selbst vor es selbst gebracht. Dieses Vor-sich-selbst-bringen von Welt ist der ursprüngliche Entwurf der Möglichkeiten des Daseins, sofern es inmitten von Seiendem zu diesem sich soll verhalten können. Der Entwurf von Welt aber ist, imgleichen wie er das Entworfene nicht eigens erfaßt, so auch immer *Überwurf* der entworfenen Welt über das Seiende. Der vorgängige Überwurf ermöglicht erst, daß Seiendes als solches sich offenbart. Dieses Geschehen des entwerfenden Überwurfs, worin sich das Sein des Daseins zeitigt, ist das In-der-Welt-sein. »Das Dasein transzendiert« heißt: es ist im Wesen seines Seins *weltbildend* und zwar »bildend« in dem mehrfachen Sinne, daß es Welt geschehen läßt, mit der Welt sich einen ursprünglichen Anblick (Bild) gibt, der nicht eigens erfaßt, gleichwohl gerade als Vor-bild für alles offenbare Seiende fungiert, darunter das jeweilige Dasein selbst gehört.

the contrary, only by elucidating transcendence can we even begin to define what "subject" and "subjective" mean. Ultimately the concept of world must be construed in such a way that the world is indeed subjective but for that very reason does not (as would a being) fall within the inner sphere of a "subjective" subject. And, by the same token, neither is the world merely objective if "objective" means "belonging among the objects that are."

As the totality of what exists for the sake of a Dasein at any given time, the world is brought by Dasein before Dasein itself. This "bringing itself before itself" of world is the primordial project of the possibilities of Dasein, insofar as Dasein can relate itself to being from within the midst of being. The project of world, though it does not grasp what is projected explicitly, does *throw* the projected world *over* being. This, in turn, allows being to manifest itself. The happening of the projecting "throwing the world over being," in which the Being of Dasein arises, we call Being-in-the-world. "Dasein transcends" means: the essence of its Being is such that it *"forms the world,"* in the sense that it lets world happen and through the world provides itself with an original view (form) which does not grasp explicitly, yet serves as a model for, all of manifest being, Dasein included. [34]

There is no way that being, or nature in the widest sense, might become manifest if it could not find the *opportunity* to enter a world. Thus we say that being can, and often does, make an *entrance into a world.* "Entering a world" is not an event that

Seiendes, etwa die Natur im weitesten Sinne, könnte in keiner Weise offenbar werden, wenn es nicht *Gelegenheit* fände, in eine Welt einzugehen. Wir sprechen daher vom möglichen und gelegentlichen *Welteingang* des Seienden. Welteingang ist kein Vorgang am eingehenden Seienden, sondern etwas, das »mit« dem Seienden »geschieht«. Und dieses Geschehen ist das Existieren von Dasein, das als existierendes transzendiert. Nur wenn in der Allheit von Seiendem das Seiende »seiender« wird in der Weise der Zeitigung von Dasein, ist Stunde und Tag des Welteingangs von Seiendem. Und nur wenn diese Urgeschichte, die Transzendenz, geschieht, d. h. wenn Seiendes vom Charakter des In-der-Welt-seins in das Seiende einbricht, besteht die Möglichkeit, daß Seiendes sich offenbart.[56]

Schon die bisherige Erhellung der Transzendenz läßt verstehen, daß sie, wenn anders in ihr allein Seiendes als Seiendes ans Licht kommen kann, einen *ausgezeichneten Bezirk* ausmacht für die Ausbildung aller Fragen, die das Seiende als solches, d. h. in seinem Sein betreffen. Bevor wir das leitende Problem des Grundes im Bezirk der Transzendenz auseinanderlegen und damit das Transzendenzproblem in einer bestimmten Hinsicht verschärfen, soll die Transzendenz des Daseins durch eine erneute historische Erinnerung noch vertrauter werden.

56. Durch die ontologische Interpretation des Daseins als In-der-Welt-sein ist weder positiv noch negativ über ein mögliches Sein zu Gott entschieden. Wohl aber wird durch die Erhellung der Transzendenz allererst ein *zureichender Begriff* des *Daseins* gewonnen, mit Rücksicht auf welches Seiende nunmehr *gefragt* werden kann, wie es mit dem Gottesverhältnis des Daseins ontologisch bestellt ist.

takes place within (or outside) the realm of being but something that "happens with" being. And this happening is the existing of Dasein which, as existing, transcends. Only if, within the totality of being, a being "is" to some greater extent because it gets involved in Dasein's temporality [35] can we speak of its "entering a world" having an hour and day. And being can manifest itself only if this prehistoric happening, which we call transcendence, happens, i.e., if being of the character of Being-in-the-world breaks into the entirety of being.[56]

The foregoing illumination of transcendence is enough to show that, to the extent that being can come to light in it, transcendence represents a *distinctive realm* for the formation of all questions concerning being as such, i.e., in its Being. Before we try to analyze the central problem of reasons within the realm of transcendence and thereby bring the problem of transcendence into focus, we should get better acquainted with the transcendence of Dasein by thinking back over the history of this concept.

56. The ontological interpretation of Dasein as Being-in-the-world tells neither for nor against the possible existence of God. One must first gain an *adequate concept* of *Dasein* by illuminating transcendence. Then, by considering Dasein, one can *ask* how the relationship of Dasein to God is ontologically constituted.

Eigens ausgesprochen ist die Transzendenz in
Platos ἐπέκεινα τῆς οὐσίας.[57] Aber läßt sich das ἀγαθόν als
die Transzendenz des *Daseins* auslegen? Schon ein
flüchtiger Blick auf den Zusammenhang, innerhalb
dessen Plato die Frage nach dem ἀγαθόν erörtert,
muß solche Bedenken zerstreuen. Das Problem des
ἀγαθόν ist nur die Aufgipfelung der zentralen und
konkreten Frage nach der führenden Grundmöglich-
keit der *Existenz des Daseins* in der Polis. Mag nun
auch die Aufgabe eines ontologischen Entwurfs des
Daseins auf seine metaphysische Grundverfassung
nicht ausdrücklich gestellt und gar ausgebildet sein,
so drängt doch die dreifache in ständiger Entsprechung zur »Sonne« durchgeführte Charakteristik
des ἀγαθόν auf die Frage nach der Möglichkeit von
Wahrheit, Verstehen und Sein—d. h. in der Zusam-
menfassung der Phänomene—auf die Frage nach
dem ursprünglicheinigen Grunde der Möglichkeit
der Wahrheit des Verstehens von Sein. Dieses Verstehen—als enthüllendes Entwerfen von Sein—ist
aber die Urhandlung menschlicher Existenz, in der
alles Existieren inmitten des Seienden gewurzelt sein
muß. Das ἀγαθόν ist nun diejenige ἕξις (Mächtigkeit),
die der Möglichkeit von Wahrheit, Verstehen und
sogar des Seins mächtig ist und zwar aller drei in
Einheit zumal.

Nicht zufällig ist das ἀγαθόν inhaltlich unbestimmt, so daß alle Definitionen und Deutungen in
dieser Hinsicht scheitern müssen. Rationalistische
Erklärungen versagen in gleicher Weise wie die
»irrationalistische« Flucht zum »Geheimnis«. Die
Aufhellung des ἀγαθόν muß entsprechend der Hinweisung, die Plato selbst gibt, sich an die Aufgabe

57. Res publ. VI, 509 B.

Transcendence is explicitly expressed in Plato's *epekeina tēs ousias* [beyond essence].[57] But can the *agathon* [good] be interpreted as the transcendence of Dasein? A brief glance at the context within which Plato discusses the question of the *agathon* is enough to show that it cannot. The problem of the *agathon* is merely the culminating point of the central, very concrete question about the basic possibility of the *existence of Dasein* in the *polis*. Even if the task of an ontological project of Dasein is not explicitly placed, or even developed, on its metaphysical foundation, the threefold characterization of the *agathon*, elaborated with constant analogy to the "sun," leads to the question about the possibility of truth, understanding, and Being—or, considering all three phenomena together, to the question about the primordial, unified ground of [reason for] the possibility of the truth of the understanding of Being. As the disclosing project of Being, this understanding is the ultimate pursuit of human existence, a pursuit in which all existing in the midst of being must be rooted. Thus the *agathon* is that *hexis* [mastery] which is master of the possibility of truth, understanding, and even of Being, indeed of all three together at once.

It is no accident that the content of the *agathon* is indefinite, so that definitions and interpretations of it must miscarry. Rationalistic explanations fail in the same way as the "irrationalistic" flight to the "secret." [36] If we wish to clarify the *agathon*, then, we should take the hint that Plato himself gives and hew to the task of interpreting the essence of the connection of truth, understanding, and Being. In-

57. *Republic* VI. 509B.

der Wesensinterpretation des Zusammenhangs von
Wahrheit, Verstehen und Sein halten. Das Zurück-
fragen in die innere Möglichkeit dieses Zusammenhangs sieht sich »gezwungen«, den Übersteig *ausdrücklich* zu vollziehen, der in jedem Dasein als
solchem notwendig aber zumeist verborgen geschieht. Das Wesen des ἀγαθόν liegt in der Mächtigkeit seiner selbst als οὗ ἕνεκα—als das *Umwillen* von
. . . ist es die Quelle von Möglichkeit als solcher.
Und weil schon das Mögliche höher liegt denn das
Wirkliche, deshalb ist gar ἡ τοῦ ἀγαθοῦ ἕξις, die We-
sensquelle von Möglichkeit, μειζόνως τιμητέον.[58]

Freilich wird gerade jetzt der Bezug des Umwillen zum Dasein problematisch. Allein dieses Problem kommt nicht an den Tag. Vielmehr bleiben
nach traditiongewordener Lehre die Ideen an einem
ὑπερουράνιος τόπος; es gilt nur, sie als das Objektivste
der Objekte, als das Seiende am Seienden, zu si-
chern, ohne daß sich dabei das Umwillen als pri-
märer Weltcharakter zeigte und so der ursprüngliche Gehalt des ἐπέκεινα als Transzendenz des Daseins zur Auswirkung käme. Umgekehrt erwacht
später nun auch die im »wiedererinnernden«
»Selbstgespräch der Seele« bei *Plato* schon vorge-
bildete Tendenz, die Ideen als dem »Subjekt« einge-
boren zu fassen. Beide Versuche bekunden, daß die
Welt dem Dasein sowohl vorgehalten (jenseitig) ist,
als auch zugleich wieder im Dasein sich selbst
bildet. Die Geschichte des Ideenproblems zeigt, wie
die Transzendenz immer schon ans Licht drängt,
aber zugleich zwischen zwei selbst unzureichend
gegründeten und bestimmten Polen der möglichen
Auslegung hin und her schwingt. Die Ideen gelten

58. A. a. O. 509 A.

quiring back into the inner possibility of this connection, we see ourselves "forced" to execute *explicitly* the surpassing that happens necessarily, though for the most part covertly, in every Dasein. The essence of the *agathon* lies in its mastery of itself as *hou heneka;* as the *"for the sake* of . . . ," it is the source of possibility as such. And because the possible is "higher" than the actual, even *hē tou agathou hexis* [the mastery of the good], i.e., the source of the essence of possibility, is *meizonōs timē-teon* [still more to be honored].[58]

Now, of course, the relationship of the "for the sake of . . ." to Dasein becomes problematic. But the problem does not come to light. According to the Platonic doctrine, since become traditional, the Ideas instead remain in a *hyperouranios topos* [place above the heavens]. Plato has merely to ensure that they will be the most objective of objects, the being of beings. The "for the sake of . . ." does not have to be revealed as the primary feature of world; the primordial content of the *epekeina* [beyond] need not work out to be the transcendence of Dasein. On the other hand, while prefigured in Plato's discussion of "the conversation that the soul holds with itself . . . in memory," [37] a tendency later arises to construe the Ideas as innate in the "subject." Both lines of interpretation agree that, even though the world is formed in Dasein, access to the world is denied Dasein on nonfinite terms. The history of the problem of the Ideas shows how transcendence continually finds its way into the picture and, at the same time, wavers between two poles of possible interpretation, each inadequately grounded

58. *Ibid.,* 509 A.

für objektiver als die Objekte und zugleich für sub-
jektiver als das Subjekt. Wie an die Stelle des nicht
wiedererkannten Weltphänomens ein ausgezeichneter Bezirk des Immerseienden tritt, so wird auch
der *Bezug* zur Welt im Sinne einer bestimmten Verhaltung zu diesem Seienden, als *νοεῖν*, intuitus, als
nicht mehr vermitteltes Vernehmen, »Vernunft«,
gedeutet. Das »transzendentale Ideal« geht zusammen mit dem intuitus originarius.

In dieser flüchtigen Erinnerung an die noch
verborgene Geschichte des ursprünglichen Tran-
szendenzproblems muß die Einsicht erwachsen,
daß die Transzendenz nicht durch eine Flucht ins
Objektive enthüllt und gefaßt werden kann, sondern
einzig durch eine ständig zu erneuernde ontologische Interpretation der Subjektivität des Subjekts,
die dem »Subjektivismus« ebenso entgegenhandelt,
wie sie dem »Objektivismus« die Gefolgschaft versagen muß.[59]

59. Hier mag der Hinweis erlaubt sein, daß das bisher
Veröffentlichte aus den Untersuchungen über »Sein und
Zeit« nichts anderes zur Aufgabe hat als einen konkret-
enthüllenden Entwurf der *Transzendenz* (vgl. §§ 12–83;
bes. § 69). Dies wiederum geschieht zur Ermöglichung der
einzig leitenden Absicht, die in der *Überschrift* des *ganzen*
ersten Teils klar angezeigt ist, den »*transzendentalen* Horizont der *Frage* nach dem Sein« zu gewinnen. Alle konkreten
Interpretationen, vor allem die der Zeit, sind *allein* in der
Richtung auf die *Ermöglichung* der Seinsfrage auszuwerten.
Sie haben mit der modernen »dialektischen Theologie« so
wenig zu tun wie mit der Scholastik des Mittelalters.
Wenn dabei das Dasein als das Seiende interpretiert
wird, das überhaupt so etwas wie ein Seinsproblem als zu
seiner Existenz gehörig stellen kann, dann heißt das *nicht,*
dieses Seiende, das *als Dasein* eigentlich und uneigentlich
existieren kann, sei *das* »eigentliche« Seiende *überhaupt*
unter allem übrigen Seienden, so daß dieses nur ein Schat-
ten von jenem wäre. Gerade im Gegenteil soll in der Auf-

and defined. The Ideas are considered more objective than objects and yet more subjective than the subject. Just as a distinctive realm of eternal being (the *hyperouranios topos*) takes the place of the unrecognized phenomenon of world, so Dasein's *relationship* to the world (in the sense of a definite way of behaving toward the entirety of being) is interpreted as *noein* or *intuitus,* as no longer mediated perception, as "Reason." [38] The "transcendental Ideal" goes together with the *intuitus originarius.*

Our brief consideration of the still-concealed history of the primordial problem of transcendence suggests that transcendence cannot be disclosed and understood through a flight to the objective, but solely through an ontological interpretation of the subjectivity of the subject: an interpretation which, if constantly renewed, will speak against "subjectivism" and, at the same time, deny "objectivism" any authority.[59]

59. We might point out here that the portion of the investigations concerning "Being and time" published so far has as its task nothing more than a concrete, revealing sketch [project] of transcendence (cf. §§ 12–83, esp. § 69). The sketch is there in order to make the *single* prominent goal of these investigations possible, a goal that is clearly indicated in the *heading* of the *whole* first part: namely, attaining the "*transcendental* horizon of the *question* about Being." All concrete interpretations, above all the interpretation of time, should be evaluated *strictly* as they aim at making the *question* of Being possible. They have no more to do with modern "dialectical theology" than with medieval scholastic theology. [39]

While Dasein is interpreted as the being which alone can pose the problem of Being as a problem of its existence, that does *not* mean that this being, which *as Dasein* can exist both authentically and inauthentically, is *the only* "real" [authentic] being out of all the rest of being or that

hellung der Transzendenz *der* Horizont gewonnen werden, in dem sich erst der Seinsbegriff—auch der viel berufene »natürliche«—*als Begriff* philosophisch begründen läßt. Ontologische Interpretation des Seins in und aus der Transzendenz des Daseins heißt aber doch nicht ontische Ableitung des Alls des nicht-daseinsmäßigen Seienden aus dem Seienden qua Dasein.

Und was dann die mit solcher Mißdeutung zusammenhängende Vorhaltung eines »anthropozentrischen Standpunktes« in »Sein und Zeit« betrifft, so bleibt dieser jetzt allzu eifrig von Hand zu Hand gereichte Einwand solange nichtssagend, als man unterläßt, im Durchdenken des Ansatzes, des *ganzen Zuges* und des *Ziels* der Problementwicklung in »Sein und Zeit« zu begreifen, wie gerade durch die Herausarbeitung der Transzendenz des Daseins »der Mensch« so ins »Zentrum« kommt, daß seine Nichtigkeit im Ganzen des Seienden allererst *Problem* werden kann und muß. Welche Gefahren birgt denn ein »anthropozentrischer Standpunkt« in sich, der gerade *alle* Bemühung *einzig* darauf legt, zu zeigen, daß das *Wesen* des Daseins, das da »im Zentrum« steht, ekstatisch, d. h. »*exzentrisch*« ist und daß deshalb aber auch die vermeintliche Standpunktsfreiheit wider allen Sinn des Philosophierens als einer wesenhaft *endlichen* Möglichkeit der Existenz ein Wahn bleibt? Vgl. hierzu die Interpretation der ekstatisch-horizontalen Struktur der Zeit als Zeitlichkeit in »Sein und Zeit« I, S. 316–438.

the latter is merely a shadow of the former. Quite the contrary, by illuminating transcendence, we are supposed to gain *the* horizon within which the concept of Being—even the much discussed "natural" concept—can alone be philosophically grounded *as a concept.* So our ontological interpretation of Being in terms of the transcendence of Dasein is by no means equivalent to the ontical derivation of the entirety of non-Daseinal from Daseinal being.

Some have advanced an objection that is based on this misunderstanding and now eagerly passed from mouth to mouth: namely, that *Sein und Zeit* works from an "anthropocentric standpoint." [40] The objection makes sense only if one fails to understand, in thinking through its point of departure, the *whole bent* and *goal* of the development of problems in *Sein und Zeit,* i.e., if one fails to understand how, by elaborating the structure of transcendence of Dasein, "man" comes into the "center" of the picture, so that his nothingness within the totality of being can and must become a problem of first priority. We should take care to ask what pitfalls lurk in the kind of "anthropocentric standpoint" which *merely* attempts to show that the essence of Dasein (which then stands "in the center") is ecstatic or *"excentric"* and, consequently, that even Dasein's alleged freedom of standpoint [41] runs against any sense of philosophizing as an essentially *finite* possibility of existence. For an analysis of the problem cf. the interpretation of the ecstatic-horizonal structure of time as temporality in *Sein und Zeit,* Part I, pp. 316–438.

III / VOM WESEN DES GRUNDES

DIE ERÖRTERUNG DES »Satzes vom Grunde« hat das Problem des Grundes in den Bezirk der Transzendenz verwiesen (I). Diese ist auf dem Wege einer Analyse des Weltbegriffes als das In-der-Welt-sein des Daseins bestimmt worden (II). Jetzt gilt es, aus der Transzendenz des Daseins das Wesen des Grundes aufzuhellen.

Inwiefern liegt in der Transzendenz die innere Möglichkeit für so etwas wie Grund überhaupt? Die Welt gibt sich dem Dasein als die jeweilige Ganzheit des Umwillen seiner, d. h. aber umwillen eines Seienden, das gleichursprünglich ist: das Sein bei . . . Vorhandenem, das Mitsein mit . . . dem Dasein Anderer und Sein zu . . . ihm selbst. Das Dasein kann in dieser Weise nur dann zu ihm als ihm selbst sein, wenn es »sich« im Umwillen übersteigt. Der umwillentliche Überstieg geschieht nur in einem »Willen«, der als solcher sich auf Möglichkeiten seiner selbst entwirft. Dieser Wille, der dem Dasein wesenhaft das Umwillen seiner über- und damit vorwirft, kann daher nicht ein bestimmtes Wollen sein, ein »Willensakt« im Unterschied zu

III / THE ESSENCE OF REASONS

OUR DISCUSSION of the "principle of sufficient reason" has referred the problem of reasons to the realm of transcendence (I). Transcendence was defined by way of an analysis of the concept of world as the Being-in-the-world of Dasein (II). We must now illuminate the essence of reasons in terms of the transcendence of Dasein.

To what extent does the inner possibility of reasons lie in transcendence? The world reveals itself to Dasein as the actual totality of what exists "for the sake of" Dasein, [42] but that means for the sake of a being that is equiprimordial with Dasein: "Being alongside . . . what is present at hand," "Being with . . . the Dasein of others," and "Being toward . . . itself." Dasein can then be toward it as itself only if it surpasses "itself" in the "for the sake of. . . ." Surpassing for the sake of something, in turn, happens only in a "will" which projects itself toward possibilities of itself and, at an essential level, throws the "for the sake of its . . ." over and to Dasein. [43] This will cannot be a specific "wanting," an "act of willing" as opposed to other kinds of

anderem Verhalten (z. B. Vorstellen, Urteilen, Sich-
freuen). Alle Verhaltungen sind in der Transzendenz verwurzelt. Jener »Wille« aber soll als und im
Überstieg das Umwillen selbst »bilden«. Was nun
aber seinem Wesen nach so etwas wie das Umwillen
überhaupt entwerfend vorwirft und nicht etwa als
gelegentliche Leistung auch hervorbringt, ist das,
was wir *Freiheit* nennen. Der Überstieg zur Welt ist
die Freiheit selbst. Demnach stößt die Transzendenz nicht auf das Umwillen als auf so etwas wie
einen an sich vorhandenen Wert und Zweck, sondern Freiheit hält sich—*und zwar als Freiheit*—das
Umwillen *entgegen*. In diesem transzendierenden
Sichentgegenhalten des Umwillen geschieht das Dasein im Menschen, so daß er im Wesen seiner
Existenz auf sich verpflichtet, d. h. ein freies Selbst
sein kann. Hierin enthüllt sich aber die Freiheit
zugleich als die Ermöglichung von Bindung und
Verbindlichkeit überhaupt. *Freiheit allein kann dem
Dasein eine Welt walten und welten lassen.* Welt
ist nie, sondern *weltet*.

Am Ende liegt in dieser aus der Transzendenz
gewonnenen Auslegung der Freiheit eine ursprünglichere Kennzeichnung ihres Wesens gegenüber
der Bestimmung derselben als Spontaneität, d. h. als
einer Art von Kausalität. Das Von-selbst-anfangen
gibt nur die negative Charakteristik der Freiheit,
daß weiter zurück keine bestimmende Ursache liege.
Diese Kennzeichnung übersieht aber vor allem, daß
sie ontologisch indifferent von »Anfangen« und
»Geschehen« spricht, ohne daß sich das Ursachesein
ausdrücklich aus der spezifischen Seinsart des *so*
Seienden, des Daseins, charakterisiert. Soll demnach die Spontaneität (»Von-selbst-anfangen«) als

behavior (e.g., representing, judging, rejoicing); every kind of behavior is rooted in transcendence. Instead it must be a "will" which, as and in surpassing, might be said to "form" or "create" the "for the sake of. . . ." That which produces and must produce the "for the sake of . . . ," throwing forth the "for the sake of . . ." in projecting, we call "freedom." Surpassing to the world is freedom itself. Thus, transcendence does not meet with the "for the sake of . . ." as a value or end, in itself present at hand. Rather, freedom holds [opposes] itself—*as freedom—over against* [*to*] the "for the sake of. . . ." Transcending and holding itself over against the "for the sake of . . . ," Dasein happens in man, so that he can be under obligation to himself in the essence of his existence, i.e., he can be a free self. Thus freedom reveals itself as that which makes bonds and obligations possible in the first place. *Freedom alone can let a world govern and "world" Dasein.* World never "is"; it "worlds." [44]

We can characterize the essence of freedom more originally by explaining it in terms of transcendence than by defining it as spontaneity, i.e., as a type of causality. To say that a free act is one that "is initiated by itself" or "begins with itself" [45] is merely to offer a negative way of characterizing freedom. It is merely to say that no determining cause can be said to lie behind the free act. Above all, it is to err on an ontological level in making no distinction between "initiating" and "happening" and in failing to characterize what it means to be "a cause" in terms of the peculiar mode of Being of the being which *exists* as cause, namely Dasein. Spontaneity ("being initiated by itself") can serve as an

Wesenscharakteristik des »Subjekts« dienen können, dann ist zuvor ein Doppeltes gefordert: 1. die
Selbstheit muß ontologisch geklärt sein für eine
mögliche angemessene Fassung des »von selbst«; 2.
ebendieselbe Klärung der Selbstheit muß die Vor-
zeichnung des *Geschehens*charakters eines Selbst
hergeben, um die Bewegungsweise des »Anfangens«
bestimmen zu können. *Die Selbstheit des aller Spontaneität schon zugrunde liegenden Selbst liegt aber
in der Transzendenz.* Das entwerfend-überwerfende
Waltenlassen von Welt ist die Freiheit. Nur weil
diese die Transzendenz ausmacht, kann sie sich im
existierenden Dasein als eine ausgezeichnete Art
von Kausalität bekunden. Die Auslegung der Freiheit als »Kausalität« bewegt sich aber vor allem
schon in einem bestimmten Verständnis von Grund.
Die Freiheit als Transzendenz ist jedoch nicht nur
eine eigene »Art« von Grund, sondern der *Ursprung
von Grund überhaupt. Freiheit ist Freiheit zum
Grunde.*

Die ursprüngliche Beziehung der Freiheit zu
Grund nennen wir das *Gründen*. Gründend *gibt* sie
Freiheit und *nimmt* sie Grund. Dieses in der Transzendenz gewurzelte Gründen ist aber in eine Mannigfaltigkeit von Weisen *gestreut*. Es sind deren
drei: 1. das Gründen als Stiften; 2. das Gründen als
Boden-nehmen; 3. das Gründen als Begründen.
Wenn diese Weisen des Gründens zur Transzendenz
gehören, dann können die Titel »Stiften«, »Boden-
nehmen«, offenbar nicht eine vulgär ontische Bedeutung, sondern müssen eine *transzendentale*
haben. Inwiefern ist aber das Transzendieren des
Daseins ein Gründen nach den genannten Weisen?

essential feature of the "subject" only on two conditions: 1. Selfhood must be ontologically clarified in order to provide an appropriate manner of reading the phrase "by itself." 2. The same clarification of selfhood, if it is to be able to define the sort of "move" involved in "initiating," must somehow explain the "eventful" character of a self. *But the selfhood of the self, which lies at the basis of all spontaneity, itself lies in transcendence.* Freedom is what lets world govern—by projecting and throwing world over being. Only because freedom constitutes transcendence can it announce itself in existing Dasein as a distinctive kind of causality. In interpreting freedom as "causality," however, we work on a peculiar understanding of reasons that precedes and suggests the interpretation. As transcendence, freedom is not merely a particular "kind" of reason but the *origin of reasons* [*grounds*] *in general. Freedom is freedom for grounds.*

The primordial relationship of freedom to grounds we call "grounding." In grounding, the relationship *offers* freedom and *takes* ground. Rooted in transcendence, grounding is *dispersed* in three ways: 1. grounding as establishing [46]; 2. grounding as obtaining a footing [47]; and 3. grounding as founding. Since all three ways of grounding belong to transcendence, the terms "establishing," "obtaining a footing," etc., obviously cannot retain their common ontical meanings but must each acquire a *transcendental* meaning. To what extent is the transcending of Dasein a grounding in the ways we have mentioned?

Als »erste« unter den Weisen wird mit Absicht das »Stiften« aufgeführt. Nicht als ob es die übrigen aus sich hervorgehen ließe. Auch ist es weder das zunächst bekannte noch gar zuerst erkannte Gründen. Gleichwohl eignet gerade ihm ein Vorrang, der sich daran zeigt, daß schon die vorstehende Erhellung der Transzendenz ihm nicht ausweichen konnte. Dieses »erste« Gründen ist nichts anderes als *der Entwurf des Umwillen.* Wenn dieses freie Waltenlassen von Welt als Transzendenz bestimmt wurde, zum Weltentwurf als Gründen aber auch die anderen Weisen des Gründens notwendig gehören, dann ergibt sich hieraus, daß bisher weder die Transzendenz noch die Freiheit zu ihrer vollen Bestimmtheit gebracht sind. Zwar liegt im Weltentwurf des Daseins immer, daß es in und durch den Überstieg auf Seiendes zurückkommt. Das im Vorwurf entworfene Umwillen weist auf das Ganze des in diesem Welthorizont enthüllbaren Seienden zurück. Zu diesem gehört jeweils, in welchen Stufen der Abhebung und Graden der Ausdrücklichkeit auch immer: Seiendes als Dasein und nichtdaseinsmäßiges Seiendes. Aber im Weltentwurf ist doch dieses Seiende an ihm selbst noch nicht offenbar. Ja es müßte verborgen bleiben, wenn nicht das entwerfende Dasein *als entwerfendes* auch schon *inmitten* von jenem Seienden wäre. Dieses »Inmitten von . . .« besagt aber weder Vorkommen unter anderem Seienden noch aber auch: sich eigens *auf* dieses Seiende, *zu* ihm sich *verhaltend,* richten. Dieses Inmittensein von . . . gehört vielmehr zur Transzendenz. Das *Über*steigende und so sich Erhöhende muß als solches im Seienden *sich befinden.* Das Dasein wird als befindliches vom Seienden

"Establishing" is purposely cited as the "first" way, though not because the others derive from it. It is neither the way of grounding we are best acquainted with, nor even the one we first know and understand. That it nevertheless enjoys a certain priority is evident from the fact that we could not avoid discussing it in the foregoing elucidation of transcendence. This "first" type of grounding is none other than the *project of the "for the sake of. . . ."* While we defined that which lets world govern freely as transcendence, the other ways of grounding must also belong to the project of world insofar as the project of world is itself a way of grounding. It follows that neither transcendence nor freedom has yet been fully defined. Dasein's project of world always returns to being in and through surpassing. The "for the sake of . . ." projects in "throwing forth" and refers back to the whole of being that can be disclosed in this world-horizon. No matter how prominent or explicit, both Daseinal and non-Daseinal being belong to this totality. But the project of world is not enough to reveal non-Daseinal being in itself. Non-Daseinal being would necessarily remain concealed if projecting Dasein were not already *in the midst* of it *as projecting*. To be "in the midst of . . ." means neither to be present among other beings nor to be prepared *for* being in *behaving toward* it. The character of "being in the midst of . . ." belongs instead to transcendence. That which surpasses and so "passes beyond" being must first be situated in the midst of being. As situated, Dasein is

eingenommen so, daß es dem Seienden zugehörig
von ihm *durchstimmt ist. Transzendenz heißt Weltentwurf, so zwar, daß das Entwerfende vom Seienden, das es übersteigt, auch schon gestimmt durchwaltet ist.* Mit solcher zur Transzendenz gehörigen
Eingenommenheit vom Seienden hat das Dasein im
Seienden Boden genommen, »Grund« gewonnen.
Dieses »zweite« Gründen entsteht nicht *nach* dem
»ersten«, sondern ist mit ihm »gleichzeitig«. Damit
ist nicht gemeint, sie seien in demselben Jetzt vorhanden, sondern: Entwurf von Welt und Eingenommenheit vom Seienden gehören als Weisen des
Gründens je zu *einer* Zeitlichkeit, sofern sie deren
Zeitigung mitausmachen. Aber gleichwie »in« der
Zeit die Zukunft vorhergeht, sich aber nur zeitigt,
sofern eben Zeit, d. h. auch Gewesenheit und Gegen-
wart in der spezifischen Zeit-Einheit sich zeitigen,
so zeigen auch die der Transzendenz entspringen-
den Weisen des Gründens diesen Zusammenhang.
Diese Entsprechung aber besteht deshalb, weil die
Transzendenz im *Wesen* der Zeit, d. h. aber in ihrer
ekstatisch-horizontalen Verfassung wurzelt.[60]

Das Dasein könnte nicht als Seiendes von Seiendem durchstimmt und demzufolge z. B. von ihm
umfangen, durch es benommen und von ihm durch-
schwungen sein, es entbehrte hierfür überhaupt des
Spielraums, wenn nicht mit dieser Eingenommenheit vom Seienden ein Aufbruch von Welt, und sei
es auch nur ein Weltdämmer, mitginge. Die enthüllte Welt mag dabei begrifflich wenig oder gar
nicht durchsichtig sein, Welt mag sogar als *ein*
Seiendes unter anderem gedeutet werden, ein aus-

---

60. Die temporale Interpretation der Transzendenz
bleibt in der vorliegenden Betrachtung durchgängig und
absichtlich beiseite.

preoccupied with being in the sense that it forms part of being; and it forms part of being in the sense that it is *disposed* and *permeated* by being. *Transcendence means project of world. As that which projects from the being which it surpasses, it is itself disposed and governed prior to projecting.* [48] By virtue of the preoccupation with being that is part of transcendence, Dasein has obtained a footing in being, or has gained "ground." This "second" type of grounding does not arise *after* the "first" but is "simultaneous" with it. This does not mean that they are present at hand at the same moment but that the project of world and preoccupation with being, as ways of grounding, belong to *one* temporality which they jointly institute. "In" time, the future is anterior and is only temporalized insofar as past and present are also temporalized in the specific unity of time; the three ways of grounding which arise from transcendence bear a corresponding relationship to one another. This correspondence exists because transcendence is rooted in the *essence* of time, i.e., in its ecstatic-horizonal constitution.[60]

If the world did not appear, or at least dawn, in Dasein's preoccupation with being, it could not as a being be disposed by being. Nor, then, could it be, for example, encompassed or stifled or permeated by being. For it would lack the necessary "leeway." Conceptually, the disclosed world may be either partially

60. In the foregoing discussion, the temporal interpretation of transcendence is completely and purposely disregarded.

drückliches Wissen um das Transzendieren des Daseins kann fehlen, die den Weltentwurf mit sich bringende Freiheit des Daseins mag kaum wach sein—das Dasein ist doch nur *als* In-der-Welt-sein vom Seienden eingenommen. Das Dasein gründet (stiftet) Welt nur als sich gründend inmitten von Seiendem.

Im stiftenden Gründen als dem Entwurf von *Möglichkeiten seiner selbst* liegt nun aber, daß sich das Dasein darin jeweils *überschwingt*. Der Entwurf von Möglichkeiten ist seinem Wesen nach jeweils reicher als der im Entwerfenden schon ruhende Besitz. Ein solcher eignet aber dem Dasein, weil es als entwerfendes sich inmitten von Seiendem befindet. Damit sind dem Dasein bereits bestimmte andere Möglichkeiten—und zwar lediglich durch seine eigene Faktizität—*entzogen*. Aber gerade dieser in der Eingenommenheit vom Seienden beschlossene *Entzug* gewisser Möglichkeiten seines In-der-Welt-sein-könnens bringt erst die »wirklich« ergreifbaren Möglichkeiten des Weltentwurfs dem Dasein als seine Welt *entgegen*. Der Entzug verschafft gerade der Verbindlichkeit des verbleibenden entworfenen Vorwurfs die Gewalt ihres Waltens im Existenzbereich des Daseins. *Die Transzendenz ist entsprechend den beiden Weisen des Gründens überschwingend-entziehend zumal*. Daß der jeweils überschwingende Weltentwurf nur im Entzug mächtig und Besitz wird, ist zugleich ein transzendentales Dokument der *Endlichkeit* der Freiheit des Daseins. Und bekundet sich hierin gar das *endliche* Wesen von Freiheit überhaupt?

Für die Auslegung des mannigfaltigen Gründens der Freiheit ist zunächst wesentlich, die in diesem

or completely opaque; it may even be interpreted as *one* being among others; we may not know anything explicit about the transcending of Dasein; the freedom of Dasein, and so the project of world, may hardly be awake. And yet it is only *as* Being-in-the-world that Dasein is preoccupied with being. Dasein grounds (establishes) world only insofar as it grounds itself in the midst of being.

As the project of *possibilities of itself,* Dasein *outstrips* itself in the kind of grounding we call establishing. The project of possibilities is, in its essence, "richer" than the possession of them; the latter rests on the former. Dasein possesses possibilities because, as projecting, it finds itself in the midst of being. Thus Dasein is from the outset *deprived of* certain other possibilities solely by virtue of its own facticity. But this very *deprivation* of certain ways of being in the world follows from its preoccupation with being; it sets the "actually" realizable possibilities of the project of world *over against* Dasein as its world. [49] And it provides the obligatory force of what is thrown forth and remains projected with the authority of its sway in Dasein's realm of existence. *In accordance with two ways of grounding, transcendence at once both outstrips and deprives.* The fact that the outstripping project of world gains power and possession only in deprivation is transcendental testimony to the *finitude* of Dasein. But does the *finite* essence of freedom announce itself in finitude at all?

To explain freedom's many ways of grounding, we must first see the *unity* of the two we have discussed so far. Their *unity* gets revealed in the

transzendentalen Einspielen von Überschwung und Entzug aufeinander zutagetretende *Einheit* der bisher besprochenen Weisen des Gründens zu sehen.

Das Dasein ist nun aber ein Seiendes, das nicht nur inmitten von Seiendem sich befindet, sondern auch *zu* Seiendem und damit auch zu ihm selbst *sich verhält.* Dieses Verhalten zum Seienden wird zunächst und zumeist sogar der Transzendenz gleichgesetzt. Ist dies auch eine Verkennung des Wesens der Transzendenz, so muß doch die transzendentale Möglichkeit des intentionalen Verhaltens *Problem* werden. Und ist gar die Intentionalität eine ausgezeichnete Verfassung der Existenz des Daseins, dann kann sie bei einer Aufhellung der Transzendenz nicht übergangen werden.

Der *Weltentwurf* ermöglicht zwar—was hier nicht gezeigt werden kann—vorgängiges Verständnis des Seins von Seiendem, ist aber selbst kein Daseinsbezug zu *Seiendem.* Die *Eingenommenheit* wiederum, die das Dasein inmitten von Seiendem (und zwar nie ohne Weltenthüllung), von ihm durchstimmt, sich befinden läßt, ist kein *Verhalten* zu Seiendem. Wohl aber sind *beide*—in ihrer gekennzeichneten Einheit—die transzendentale Ermöglichung der Intentionalität, so zwar, daß sie dabei als Weisen des Gründens eine *dritte* mitzeitigen: *das Gründen als Be-gründen.* In diesem übernimmt die Transzendenz des Daseins die Ermöglichung des Offenbarmachens von Seiendem an ihm selbst, die Möglichkeit der ontischen Wahrheit.

»Begründen« soll hier nicht in dem engen und abgeleiteten Sinne des Beweisens ontisch-theoretischer Sätze genommen werden, sondern in einer grundsätzlich ursprünglichen Bedeutung. Darnach

way outstripping and deprivation complement each other.

Dasein is a being that not only finds itself in the midst of being but also *behaves toward* being and thereby toward itself. Its behavior toward being is usually equated with transcendence. Assuming that the equation involves a misunderstanding of the essence of transcendence, the transcendental possibility of intentional behavior must become a *problem*. And if intentionality is somehow a distinctive feature of the existence of Dasein, it cannot be ignored in elucidating transcendence. [50]

Though we cannot show why here, the *project of world* makes a preliminary understanding of the Being of being possible and yet is not itself a relationship of Dasein to *being*. Dasein, because of its *preoccupation* with being, can find itself disposed by and in the midst of being, though indeed never without a disclosure of world. But its preoccupation is not a way of *behaving* toward being. On the contrary, *both* Dasein's understanding of and its preoccupation with being—in their unity as characterized above—make intentionality transcendentally possible. As ways of grounding, then, they together give rise to a *third: grounding as founding*. In founding, the transcendence of Dasein takes charge of making the manifestation of being possible, i.e., it takes charge of the possibility of ontical truth.

"Founding" should be understood, not in the narrow and derivative sense of "proving" ontical or theoretical propositions, but in a basically primordial sense. Founding is *that which makes the question "Why?" possible in the first place*. So to clarify the

besagt Begründung soviel wie *Ermöglichung der Warumfrage überhaupt.* Den eigenen ursprünglich gründenden Charakter des Begründens sichtbar machen, heißt darnach, den transzendentalen Ursprung des Warum als solchen aufhellen. Gesucht sind also nicht etwa die Veranlassungen dafür, daß im Dasein die Warumfrage faktisch aufbricht, sondern gefragt ist nach der *transzendentalen* Möglichkeit des Warum überhaupt. Daher ist die Transzendenz selbst, soweit sie durch die beiden bisher besprochenen Weisen des Gründens bestimmt wurde, zu befragen. Das stiftende Gründen gibt als Weltentwurf Möglichkeiten der Existenz vor. Existieren besagt immer: inmitten von Seiendem befindlich zu Seiendem—zu nicht-daseinsmäßigem, zu sich selbst und seinesgleichen—sich verhalten, so zwar, daß es in diesem befindlichen Verhalten um das Seinkönnen des Daseins selbst geht. Im Weltentwurf ist ein Überschwung von Möglichem gegeben, im Hinblick worauf und im Durchwaltetsein von dem in der Befindlichkeit umdrängenden Seienden (Wirklichen) das Warum entspringt.

Weil aber die beiden zuerst aufgeführten Weisen des Gründens in der Transzendenz *zusammengehören,* ist das Entspringen des Warum ein transzendental notwendiges. Mit seinem Ursprung vermannigfaltigt sich auch schon das Warum. Die Grundformen sind: warum *so* und nicht anders? Warum dies und nicht jenes? *Warum überhaupt etwas und nicht nichts?* In diesem nach welchen Weisen immer ausgesprochenen Warum liegt aber schon ein wenngleich vorbegriffliches Vorverständnis vom Was-sein, Wie-sein und Sein (Nichts) überhaupt. Dieses Seinsverständnis ermöglicht erst das Warum.

peculiar, primordially grounding character of founding means to elucidate the transcendental origin of the Why as such. We are not looking for what gives rise, factically, to the question "Why?" in Dasein. We are inquiring after the *transcendental* possibility of the Why in the first place. Thus transcendence itself, at least insofar as it has been defined by the two ways of grounding that we have already discussed, is what we must investigate. As the project of world, the kind of grounding we call "establishing" offers possibilities of existence. For Dasein, to exist means to behave toward being while situated in the midst of being. It means to behave toward being that is not like Dasein, toward itself and toward being like itself, so that what is at issue in its situated behaving is the way Dasein can be. The project of world outstrips the possible; the Why arises in this outstripping and is governed by being (reality), which itself presses around Dasein in its situatedness.

But because the first two ways of grounding *belong together* in transcendence, the Why arises of transcendental necessity. The Why even proliferates at its very source. Its basic forms are: "Why thus and not otherwise?", "Why this and not that?", *"Why anything at all and not nothing?"* A preconceptual, prior understanding of what something is, of how it is, and even of Being (Nothing) lies implicit in the Why, no matter how it is expressed. This understanding of Being makes the Why possible in the first place. That is, it contains the ultimate and primordial answer to every question. As the most primary *answer,* the understanding of Being

Das besagt aber: es enthält schon die erst-letzte Urantwort für alles Fragen. Das Seinsverständnis gibt als vorgängigste *Antwort* schlechthin die erst-letzte *Begründung*. In ihm ist die Transzendenz als solche begründend. Weil darin Sein und Seinsverfassung enthüllt werden, heißt das transzendentale Begründen die *ontologische Wahrheit*.

Dieses Begründen liegt allem Verhalten zu Seiendem »zugrunde«, so zwar, daß erst in der Helle des Seinsverständnisses Seiendes an ihm selbst (d. h. *als* das Seiende, das es ist und wie es ist) offenbar werden kann. Weil nun aber alles Offenbarwerden von Seiendem (ontische Wahrheit) von vornherein transzendental durchwaltet ist von dem gekennzeichneten *Begründen,* deshalb muß alles ontische Entdecken und Erschließen in seiner Weise »begründend« sein, d. h. es muß sich *ausweisen.* In der Ausweisung vollzieht sich die jeweils vom Was- und Wiesein des betreffenden Seienden und der zugehörigen *Enthüllungsart* (Wahrheit) geforderte *Anführung des Seienden,* das sich dann z. B. als »Ursache« oder als »Beweggrund« (Motiv) für einen schon offenbaren Zusammenhang von Seiendem bekundet. Weil die Transzendenz des Daseins als entwerfend-befindliche, Seinsverständnis ausbildend, begründet, und weil *dieses* Gründen in der Einheit der Transzendenz mit den beiden erstgenannten gleichursprünglich ist, d. h. der endlichen Freiheit des Daseins entspringt, deshalb *kann* das Dasein in seinen faktischen Ausweisungen und Rechtfertigungen sich der »Gründe« entschlagen, den Anspruch auf sie niederhalten, sie verkehren und verdecken. Diesem Ursprung der Begründung und damit auch der Ausweisung zufolge bleibt es im

lays the ultimate *foundation* for all inquiry. In it, transcendence is *founding*. And since Being and its constitution are disclosed in transcendence, transcendental founding is called *ontological truth*.

Founding lies "at the basis" of every kind of behavior toward being. Indeed, it is only in the light of the understanding of Being that being can become manifest in itself, i.e., *as* the being that it is, and in the way it is. Because every instance of being's "becoming manifest" (ontical truth) is, from the start, transcendentally governed by founding, every instance of ontical discovering and revealing must also be "founding," i.e., must be *proved*. In proving any given instance, we *single out the particular being* that is discovered or revealed in the way prescribed by its essence and mode and by its peculiar *kind of disclosure* (truth). [51] The being will then announce itself as, for example, "cause" or "incentive" (motive) for an ontical association of being which is already manifest. Projecting and situated, transcendence shapes and develops our understanding of Being. Because it founds and because within the unity of transcendence "founding" is just as primordial as the other two ways of grounding, i.e., arises from the finite freedom of Dasein, Dasein *can* do without "reasons," or "grounds," in proving and justifying things in the course of everyday events. For that matter, Dasein can renounce its claim to them, can distort and conceal them. Because of the peculiar origin of founding, and so of proof, we sometimes overlook the freedom of Dasein —however far the range of freedom is extended,

Dasein jeweils der Freiheit überlassen, wie weit die Ausweitung getrieben wird und ob sie sich gar zur eigentlichen Begründung, d. h. Enthüllung ihrer transzendentalen Möglichkeit versteht. Wenngleich in der Transzendenz immer Sein enthüllt ist, es bedarf hierzu doch nicht der ontologisch-begrifflichen Erfassung. So kann denn überhaupt die Transzendenz *als solche* verborgen bleiben und nur in einer »indirekten« Auslegung bekannt sein. Enthüllt ist sie aber auch dann, weil sie gerade Seiendes in der Grundverfassung des In-der-Welt-seins aufgebrochen sein läßt, worin sich die Selbstenthüllung der Transzendenz bekundet. Eigens aber enthüllt sich die Transzendenz als Ursprung des Gründens, wenn dieses in seiner Dreifachheit zum *Entspringen* gebracht wird. Demnach besagt Grund: *Möglichkeit, Boden, Ausweis*. Das dreifach gestreute Gründen der Transzendenz erwirkt ursprünglich einigend erst das Ganze, in dem je ein Dasein soll existieren können. Freiheit ist in dieser dreifachen Weise Freiheit zum Grunde. Das Geschehen der Transzendenz als Gründen ist das Sichbilden des Einbruchspielraums für das jeweilige faktische *Sichhalten* des faktischen Daseins inmitten des Seienden im Ganzen.

Beschränken wir demnach die überlieferte Vierzahl der Gründe auf drei oder decken sich die drei Weisen des Gründens mit den drei Abwandlungen des πρῶτον ὅθεν bei *Aristoteles*? So äußerlich läßt sich der Vergleich nicht anstellen; denn es ist das Eigentümliche der ersten Herausstellung der »vier Gründe«, daß dabei noch nicht grundsätzlich zwischen den transzendentalen Gründen und den spezifisch ontischen Ursachen unterschieden wird. Jene sind nur das »Allgemeinere« zu diesen. Die Ur-

and whether or not it is amenable to authentic founding, i.e., to disclosure of its transcendental possibility. While Being is always disclosed in transcendence, we need not grasp it in an ontological or conceptual fashion for it to be disclosed. Transcendence can remain largely concealed *as such* and come to our attention only by way of "indirect" explanation. [52] Yet even then it is disclosed, since it allows being to appear in the basic constitution of Being-in-the-world, precisely where transcendence discloses itself in the first place. Transcendence discloses itself uniquely as the origin of grounding where grounding is brought to pass in its three ways. Thus "ground" or "reason" means: *possibility, basis,* and *proof*. Dispersed in three ways, the grounding of transcendence alone produces and primordially unifies the totality in which a Dasein must be able to exist. Freedom is, in this threefold manner, freedom for grounds. When transcendence happens as grounding, an entryway into being is formed for the factical *behavior* of factical Dasein in the midst of being in its totality.

Have we reduced the four traditional types of grounds to three, or do the three ways of grounding coincide with Aristotle's three kinds of *prōton hothen*? The comparison with Aristotle cannot be made so superficially, for what is unique about his exposition of the "four causes" is that it contains no distinction between transcendental grounds and ontical causes. The former are merely "more general" than the latter. The primordiality of transcendental grounds and their peculiar character as

sprünglichkeit der transzendentalen Gründe und ihr
spezifischer *Grund*charakter bleiben noch unter der
formalen Charakteristik der »ersten« und »obersten«
Anfänge verdeckt. Deshalb mangelt ihnen auch die
Einheit. Sie kann nur in der Gleichursprünglichkeit
des transzendentalen Ursprungs des dreifachen
Gründens bestehen. Das Wesen »des« Grundes läßt
sich nicht einmal suchen, geschweige denn finden
dadurch, daß nach einer allgemeinen Gattung gefragt wird, die sich auf dem Wege einer »Abstrak-
tion« ergeben soll. *Das Wesen des Grundes ist die
transzendental entspringende dreifache Streuung
des Gründens in Weltentwurf, Eingenommenheit
im Seienden und ontologische Begründung des
Seienden.*

Und einzig deshalb erweist sich schon das
früheste Fragen nach dem Wesen des *Grundes* als
verschlungen mit der Aufgabe einer Erhellung des
Wesens von *Sein* und *Wahrheit*.

Aber läßt sich nicht doch immer noch fragen,
warum diese drei zusammengehörigen Bestim-
mungsstücke der Transzendenz mit dem gleichen
Titel »Gründen« bezeichnet werden? Besteht hier
nur noch eine künstlich erzwungene und spielerische
Gemeinsamkeit des Wortlauts? Oder sind die drei
Weisen des Gründens doch noch in *einer* Hinsicht
—obzwar dies je wieder anders—identisch? Diese
Frage ist in der Tat zu bejahen. Die Aufhellung *der*
Bedeutung aber, hinsichtlich deren sich die drei un-
zertrennlichen Weisen des Gründens einheitlich und
doch gestreut entsprechen, läßt sich in der »Ebene«
der jetzigen Betrachtung nicht durchführen. Andeu-
tungsweise genüge der Hinweis, daß Stiftung,
Boden-nehmen und Rechtgebung je in ihrer Weise

grounds remain hidden in Aristotle's formal characterization of the "first" and "highest" beginnings. Thus they even lack a unity. Their unity can only consist in the equiprimordiality of the transcendental origin of the three ways of grounding. The essence of grounds cannot be sought, much less found, by inquiring after or trying to "abstract" a universal genus. *The essence of grounds [reasons] is the threefold transcendental dispersion of grounding in the project of world, preoccupation with being, and the ontological founding of being.*

And, for this reason alone, even the earliest inquiry about the essence of *grounds* proves to be tied up with the task of illuminating the essence of *Being* and *truth*.

But can we not ask why the three ways of grounding, which belong together and together define transcendence, are denoted by the same term? Is it simply a matter of a contrived similarity of wording? Or are the three ways of grounding identical in only *one* respect? The last question ought to be answered in the affirmative. At our present "level" of inquiry, however, we cannot elucidate *the* meaning of grounding in terms of which the three ways of grounding correspond to one another both in unity and in dispersion. To hint at this meaning, it is enough to point out that "establishing," "obtaining a footing," and "justification" *arise,* each after its own fashion, *from the care of existence and permanence,* [53] which itself is possible only as temporality.

Turning away from this problematic realm and looking back to our point of departure, we should

der Sorge der Beständigkeit und des Bestandes ent-
springen, die selbst wiederum nur als Zeitlichkeit
möglich ist.

In der geflissentlichen Abkehr von diesem Pro-
blembezirk und vielmehr rückblickend auf den Ausgang der Untersuchung soll jetzt kurz erörtert werden, ob etwas und was für das Problem des »Satzes
vom Grunde« durch die versuchte Erhellung des
»Wesens« des Grundes gewonnen ist. Der Satz
besagt: alles Seiende hat seinen Grund. Durch das
Vorstehende wird zunächst aufgehellt, *warum* das
so ist. Weil Sein »von Hause aus« als vorgängig ver-
standenes ursprünglich *begründet,* meldet jedes
Seiende als Seiendes in seiner Art »Gründe« an,
mögen diese eigens erfaßt und angemessen bestimmt werden oder nicht. Weil »Grund« ein transzendentaler Wesenscharakter des *Seins überhaupt*
ist, deshalb gilt vom *Seienden* der Satz des Grundes.
Zum Wesen des Seins aber gehört Grund, weil es
Sein (nicht Seiendes) nur gibt in der Transzendenz
als dem weltentwerfend befindlichen Gründen.

Sodann ist bezüglich des Satzes vom Grunde
deutlich geworden, daß der »Geburtsort« dieses
Prinzips weder im Wesen der Aussage noch in der
Aussagewahrheit, sondern in der ontologischen
Wahrheit, d. h. aber in der Transzendenz selbst
liegt. *Die Freiheit ist der Ursprung des Satzes vom*
Grunde; denn in ihr, der Einheit von Überschwung
und Entzug, gründet sich das als ontologische Wahrheit sich ausbildende Begründen.

Von diesem Ursprung herkommend, verstehen
wir nicht nur den Satz in seiner inneren Möglichkeit, sondern wir bekommen auch ein Auge für das
Merkwürdige und bislang Unaufgehellte seiner Fas-

briefly discuss whether we have made any progress —and, if any, what kind of progress—with the problem of the "principle of sufficient reason" by illuminating the "essence" of reasons. The principle says that every being has its grounds or reason. The foregoing remarks clarify, in an introductory way, *why* this is so. Since, from the beginning, Being (as something understood prior to inquiry or discussion) *founds* primordially, every being announces its "reasons," whether or not they are grasped explicitly and are properly defined. Because "reasons" are a transcendental, essential character of *Being*, the principle of sufficient reason is valid for every *being*. Yet "reasons" belong to the essence of Being, because "there is" Being (not being) only in transcendence as world-projecting and situated grounding.

Thus we see that the "birthplace" of the principle of sufficient reason lies neither in the essence of the assertion nor in its truth but rather in ontological truth, i.e., in transcendence itself. *Freedom is the origin of the principle of sufficient reason.* For founding, expressing itself as ontological truth, is grounded in freedom, the unity of outstripping and deprivation.

Working from this base, we not only understand the inner possibility of the principle of sufficient reason, but we also get a sense for what is remarkable about it, what has long been unclarified in all its versions and suppressed in its most common formulation. We can find renderings of the principle in Leibniz that emphasize a seemingly unimportant feature of its content. [54] Run together schematically, they read: "A reason is why this exists *rather*

sungen, das in der vulgären Formel allerdings unterdrückt ist. Gerade bei *Leibniz* finden sich Prägungen des Satzes, die einem scheinbar unerheblichen Moment seines Gehalts Ausdruck geben. In schematischer Zusammenstellung lauten sie: ratio est cur hoc *potius* existit quam aliud; ratio est cur sic *potius* existit quam aliter; ratio est cur aliquid *potius* existit quam nihil. Das »cur« äußert sich als »cur potius quam«. Auch hier ist nicht das erste Problem, auf welchem Wege und mit welchen Mitteln diese jeweils faktisch in ontischen Verhaltungen gestellten Fragen zur Entscheidung zu bringen seien. Der Aufklärung bedarf vielmehr, woran es liegt, daß sich überhaupt dem »cur« das »potius quam« sich hat beigesellen können.

Jede Ausweisung muß sich in einem Umkreis von *Möglichem* bewegen, weil sie als intentionale Verhaltung zu Seiendem hinsichtlich ihrer Möglichkeit schon einer ausdrücklichen oder unausdrücklichen (ontologischen) Begründung botmäßig ist. Diese gibt ihrem Wesen nach notwendig immer *Ausschlagbereiche* von Möglichem vor—wobei sich der Möglichkeitscharakter gemäß der Seinsverfassung des zu enthüllenden Seienden abwandelt—weil das Sein (Seinsverfassung), das begründet, als transzendentale Verbindlichkeit für das Dasein in dessen *Freiheit* gewurzelt ist. Der Widerschein *dieses* Ursprungs des Wesens von Grund im Gründen der endlichen Freiheit zeigt sich im »potius quam« der Formeln des Satzes vom Grunde. Aber wieder drängt die Erhellung der konkreten transzendentalen Zusammenhänge zwischen »Grund« und »eher als« zur Aufklärung der Idee des Seins überhaupt (Was- und Wiesein, Etwas, Nichts und Nichtigkeit).

than something else; a reason is why something exists in this way *rather* than otherwise; a reason is why anything exists *rather* than nothing." The "why" is expressed as "why rather than." The main problem here is not to decide in what way and by what means these questions, which are constantly posed factically in ontical types of behavior, might be resolved. What needs to be clarified is how, by what right, Leibniz could have connected the "rather than" with the "why" in the first place.

Every proof must move within a circle of *what is possible*, since, as intentional behavior toward being with regard to its possibility, the proof may be subjected to explicit or inexplicit (ontological) founding. By its very essence, ontological founding opens *marginal realms* of the possible—within which the character of possibility varies with the constitution of the Being of the being that is disclosed—because Being (the constitution of Being), as something that founds and as a transcendental obligation for Dasein, is rooted in Dasein's *freedom*. That the essence of grounds, or reasons, originates *here*, in the grounding of finite freedom, is intimated in the "rather than" of Leibniz' several versions of the principle of sufficient reason. But here again, illuminating the concrete transcendental connections between "reason" and "rather than" requires that we clarify the idea of Being (something, what it is, how it is, nothing, and nothingness).

Seiner überlieferten Form und Rolle nach ist der Satz vom Grunde in der Veräußerlichung haften geblieben, die eine erste Aufhellung alles »Grundsätzlichen« notwendig mit sich führt. Denn auch den Satz zu einem »Grundsatz« erklären und ihn etwa noch mit dem Satz der Identität und des Widerspruchs zusammenstellen oder gar aus diesem ableiten, führt nicht in den Ursprung, sondern kommt einem Abschneiden alles weiteren Fragens gleich. Hierbei ist überdies zu beachten, daß auch die Sätze der Identität und des Widerspruchs nicht nur *auch transzendentale* sind, sondern auf Ursprünglicheres zurückweisen, was nicht Satzcharakter hat, vielmehr zum Geschehen der Transzendenz als solcher (Zeitlichkeit) gehört.

Und so treibt denn auch der Satz vom Grunde sein Unwesen mit dem Wesen des Grundes und hält in der sanktionierten Gestalt des Grundsatzes eine ihn selbst erst auflockernde Problematik nieder. Allein dieses »Unwesen« fällt nicht etwa der vermeintlichen »Oberflächlichkeit« einzelner Philosophen zur Last und kann daher auch nicht durch ein vermeintlich radikaleres »Weiterkommen« überwunden werden. Der Grund hat sein Un-wesen, weil er der endlichen Freiheit entspringt. Diese selbst kann sich dem, was ihr so entspringt, nicht entziehen. Der transzendierend entspringende Grund legt sich auf die Freiheit selbst zurück, und sie wird *als Ursprung* selbst zum »Grund«. *Die Freiheit ist der Grund des Grundes.* Das freilich nicht im Sinne einer formalen, endlosen »Iteration«. Das Grund-sein der Freiheit hat nicht—was zu meinen sich aber immer nahelegt—den Charakter *einer* der Weisen des Gründens, sondern bestimmt sich als die gründende Einheit der transzendentalen Streuung des Gründens. Als *dieser* Grund aber ist die Freiheit der

Cast in its traditional form and role, the principle of sufficient reason has remained shackled by the superficiality that is necessarily involved in a preliminary effort at clarifying any "basic principle." To label the principle of sufficient reason "basic" or to lump it together with the principles of identity and contradiction, or even to derive it from the latter, will not lead us to its origin but call a halt to further inquiry. We should note that even the principles of identity and contradiction are not merely "also transcendental" but refer back to something more primordial, something which does not have the character of a principle but belongs to the happening of transcendence as such, namely, temporality.

And so even the principle of sufficient reason breeds confusion [55] about the essence of reasons and, disguised in the sanctioned form of a basic principle, suppresses the very set of problems that unlocks it in the first place. This confusion should not be laid to the alleged "superficiality" of individual philosophers, and therefore cannot be overcome by an allegedly more radical "departure." [56] Reasons have their confusing aspects—they may have no essence—because they arise from finite freedom; the latter cannot rid itself of what arises from it. Reasons, which have their origin in transcendence, fall back on freedom, which, *as origin,* itself becomes a "reason." *Freedom is the reason for reasons.* Not, of course, in the sense of a formal, endless "iteration." [57] Freedom is not a reason in any *one* of the ways of grounding, as we are always inclined to think, but is the grounding unity of the transcendental dispersion of grounding. As *this* kind of

Ab-grund des Daseins. Nicht als sei die einzelne freie Verhaltung grundlos, sondern die Freiheit stellt in ihrem Wesen als Transzendenz das Dasein als Seikönnen in Möglichkeiten, die vor seiner endlichen Wahl, d. h. in seinem Schicksal aufklaffen.

Aber das Dasein muß im weltentwerfenden Überstieg des Seienden sich selbst übersteigen, um *sich* aus dieser Erhöhung allererst als Abgrund verstehen zu können. Und diese Abgründigkeit des Daseins wiederum ist nichts, was einer Dialektik oder psychologischen Zergliederung sich öffnete. Das Aufbrechen des Abgrundes in der gründenden Transzendenz ist vielmehr die Urbewegung, die die Freiheit mit uns selbst vollzieht und uns damit »zu verstehen gibt«, d. h. als ursprünglichen Weltgehalt vorgibt, daß dieser, je ursprünglicher er gegründet wird, um so einfacher das Herz des Daseins, seine Selbstheit im Handeln trifft. Das Unwesen des Grundes wird sonach nur im faktischen Existieren »überwunden«, aber nie beseitigt.

Wird jedoch die Transzendenz im Sinne der Freiheit zum Grunde erstlich und letztlich als Abgrund verstanden, dann verschärft sich damit auch das Wesen dessen, was die *Eingenommenheit* des Daseins im und vom Seienden genannt wurde. Das Dasein ist—obzwar inmitten von Seiendem befindlich und von ihm durchstimmt—*als freies* Seinkönnen unter das Seiende *geworfen.* Daß es der Möglichkeit nach ein Selbst und dieses faktisch je entsprechend seiner Freiheit ist, *daß* die Transzendenz als Urgeschehen sich zeitigt, steht nicht in der Macht dieser Freiheit selbst. Solche Ohnmacht (Ge-

reason, however, freedom is the "abyss" of Dasein, its groundless or absent ground. [58] It is not as though the only kind of free behavior were groundless [unmotivated] behavior. Instead, as transcendence, freedom provides Dasein, as "potentiality for being," with possibilities which gape open before its finite choice, i.e., in its destiny.

While surpassing being in projecting its world, Dasein must surpass itself in order, from this height, to be able to understand *itself* as groundless. Its ungrounded character, however, does not lend itself to a dialectic or to psychological analysis. The appearance of the groundless in grounding transcendence is instead the primordial "move" which freedom makes with us. It is the move whereby freedom "gives us to understand"—as part of what it means to be contained in a world—that, the more primordially the contents of the world are grounded, the more readily the heart of Dasein can find its selfhood in dealing with the world. The confusion and abuse of reasons are, then, only "overcome" in factical existing; they are never eliminated.

But if transcendence (in the sense of freedom for grounds) is ultimately understood as groundless, the essence of what we called the *preoccupation* of Dasein in and with being is brought into focus. Though situated in the midst of being and disposed by it, Dasein is *thrown* among beings *as free* "potentiality for being." What does not stand within the power of freedom is *that* Dasein is a self by virtue of its possibility—a factical self because it is free— and *that* transcendence comes about as a primordial happening. This sort of powerlessness (thrownness) is not due to the fact that being infects Da-

worfenheit) aber ist nicht erst das Ergebnis des Ein-
dringens von Seiendem auf das Dasein, sondern sie
bestimmt dessen Sein als solches. Aller Weltentwurf
ist daher *geworfener*. Die Klärung des *Wesens der
Endlichkeit* des Daseins aus dessen Seinsverfassung
muß voraufgehen aller »selbstverständlichen« Ansetzung der endlichen »Natur« des Menschen, aller
Beschreibung der aus der Endlichkeit erst folgenden
Eigenschaften, vollends auch aller übereilten »Er-
klärung« der ontischen Herkunft derselben.

Das Wesen der Endlichkeit des Daseins enthüllt
sich aber in der *Transzendenz als der Freiheit zum
Grunde*.

Und so ist der Mensch, als existierende Transzendenz überschwingend in Möglichkeiten, ein
Wesen der Ferne. Nur durch ursprüngliche Fernen,
die er sich in seiner Transzendenz zu allem Seienden bildet, kommt in ihm die wahre Nähe zu den
Dingen ins Steigen. Und nur das Hörenkönnen in
die Ferne zeitigt dem Dasein als Selbst das Erwa-
chen der Antwort des Mitdaseins, im Mitsein mit
dem es die Ichheit darangeben kann, um sich als
eigentliches Selbst zu gewinnen.

sein; rather it defines the very Being of Dasein. Every project of world, then, is *thrown*. We must clarify the *essence of the finitude* of Dasein in terms of the constitutive features of its Being before proceeding to any "self-evident" definition of the finite "nature" of man, any description of those characteristics which follow from finitude alone, and certainly any hasty "explanation" of the ontical heritage of finitude.

For, in *transcendence*, the essence of the finitude of Dasein discloses itself *as freedom for reasons*.

And so man, as existing transcendence abounding in and surpassing toward possibilities, is a *creature of distance*. Only through the primordial distances he establishes toward all being in his transcendence does a true nearness to things flourish in him. And only the knack for hearing into the distance awakens Dasein as self to the answer of its Dasein with others. For only in its Dasein with others can Dasein surrender its individuality in order to win itself as an authentic self.

Critical Notes

[1] For (*ontologische*) *Differenz* cf. Heidegger, *Identität und Differenz* (Pfullingen, 1957), pp. 46–73.

[2] The verb *wesen* is seldom used outside poetry. It means "to be," but—with overtones of "live," "flourish," and "endure"—in a sense somewhat narrower and more declarative than *sein*. While Heidegger clearly writes with the poetic sense in mind, he also means to play on the cognate noun *Wesen* ("essence"); hence our translation, ". . . reveal its essence." For a full discussion of the verb cf. Heidegger, *Unterwegs zur Sprache* (Pfullingen, 1959), p. 201.

[3] *Grund* has a wide range of meanings, most of them adequately expressed in its derivatives or in other German words: "reason," "cause" (*Ursache*), "basis" (*Grundlage* or *Basis*), "motive" (*Beweggrund* or *Motiv*), "origin" (*Ursprung*), "foundation" (*Gründung* or *Grundlegung*). "Reason," as in the phrase "the reason he came," would be the best translation, except that in philosophical contexts it can too easily be understood in the sense of a faculty or mental process—a sense reserved for the word *Vernunft*. To avoid such a confusion, we have abandoned Heidegger's singular as often as possible and, in the first two sections, have written

"reasons" for *Grund;* in the last, due to the presence of the verbs *gründen* ("ground") and *begründen* ("found"), we have written "grounds." Where *Grund* occurs as a prefix, for example in *Grundcharakter* and *Grundsatz,* it translates as "basic (character/principle)."

[4] *Der Satz vom Grunde,* literally "the principle of the reason," is the German expression that Leibniz used to render the Latin, *principium rationis sufficientis. Satz* can, as in the following paragraph, also mean "proposition" or "sentence."

[5] Heidegger's choice of word is not derogatory, but a reference to Kant's saying: "One cannot learn philosophy, rather only to philosophize."

[6] The verb *erörtern* normally means "to discuss." It is worth keeping in mind, however, that Heidegger often uses the term in a special sense, explained in *Unterwegs zur Sprache,* p. 37, and roughly conveyed in the expression "consider where and how something is situated" (otherwise: *den Ort von etwas beachten*).

[7] The preposition *von* can mean "from" or "of" as well as "concerning." The clause ". . . des *Bezirks,* innerhalb dessen *vom* Wesen des Grundes gehandelt werden soll" might, then, also be translated ". . . the *realm* within which we should work *from* the essence of reasons"—not a contradictory reading, and one which we may assume Heidegger's italics are meant to suggest.

[8] Cf. note 55, below.

[9] In *Der Satz vom Grund,* published in 1957, Heidegger expresses some misgivings about the foregoing passage ("The principle states . . . obvious to everyone"). He writes that the remarks are misleading in their implication that the principle of sufficient reason, because it is a statement about being, cannot serve as our point of departure in discussing the character of reasons:

The remarks remain correct. Nonetheless, they can lead us into error [*Irre*]. Error, on the one hand, about the avenue of approach that the principle of sufficient reason offers to the question regarding the essence of reasons, and, on the other hand, about the sensibility that inspires all thought and in whose service the book tries to place itself. What is, then, misleading? How can remarks which are quite correct nonetheless be misleading? We might answer: in a simple and therefore doubly misleading way, in a way that thought is misled quite often. . . . This treatise [*Vom Wesen des Grundes*] takes it to be self-evident that the principle, "Nothing is without a reason," states something about being but fails to shed light on what it means to be a "reason." This interpretation of the principle does not even get at what is most obvious about it. Instead it takes a step which, though almost unavoidable, is too hasty. We can characterize that step in the form of an inference: since the principle of sufficient reason is a statement about being, it gives us no information about the essence of reasons (pp. 85–86).

Heidegger thinks that the inference is wrong; throughout *Der Satz vom Grund,* he uses the principle as an expression of the understanding of "Being," and of reasons, peculiar to the stage of Western philosophy that he calls "metaphysics."

[10] The preposition *über* can mean both "over" or "above" and "about" or "concerning." Throughout the following paragraph Heidegger puns on the two senses, apparently with the thought that the principle of sufficient reason, as the most general or "most over" (*oberste,* superlative of *über*: "supreme") statement that can be made about being, is also the statement that is somehow "most about" being.

[11] Following Wolff, the "School metaphysicians" (cf. note 29, below) claimed that the principle of sufficient reason is an axiom, not of logic, but of ontology. The Kantians, notably Kiesewetter and Schultze, reversed the relationship, arguing that the School had

confused "cause" and "reason" and, to that extent, the principles of causality and sufficient reason.

[12] *Übereinstimmung* ("correspondence") is hyphenated to indicate its kinship with *Einstimmigkeit* ("consonance"). Both words derive from the same root, *einstimmig*, meaning "unanimous" or, more literally, "of/for one voice (*Stimme*)."

[13] Heidegger states that something is "ontic" if it has to do with "being" (*Seiendes*), ontological if it has to do with "Being" (*Sein*) or Dasein's understanding of Being.

[14] "Factical" (*faktisch*) means "contingent" in the sense that only Dasein can be said to be "contingent." When Heidegger is discussing the "contingency" of objects, he writes *tatsächlich*. Cf. *Sein und Zeit,* §§ 38–41.

[15] The term "unconcealedness" (*Unverborgenheit*) is introduced in *Sein und Zeit,* § 44. For its meanings in Heidegger's work since 1929 cf. *Vorträge und Aufsätze* (Pfullingen, 1954), pp. 247–59, and *Holzwege* (Frankfurt, 1950), pp. 25–68.

[16] The foregoing remarks are directed at Nicolai Hartmann's *Grundzüge einer Metaphysik der Erkenntnis* (Berlin, 1921). When Heidegger talks of the "reality of the external world" in the following sentence, he is probably referring to Wilhelm Dilthey's "Beiträge zur Lösung der Frage vom Ursprung unseres Glaubens an die Realität der Aussenwelt und seinem Recht," in his *Gesammelte Schriften* (Leipzig, 1921–35), Volume V, Part I. Both texts were criticized in similar terms in *Sein und Zeit,* pp. 205 (footnote) and 208 (footnote).

[17] Husserl wrote that certain aspects of every conscious experience are "intentional" in the sense that they "constitute" (*konstituieren*) or "give meaning to" the object(s) of the experience. Heidegger's comment here is more fully elaborated in his letter to Husserl regarding the latter's *Encyclopaedia Britannica* article:

". . . daß die Existenzverfassung des Daseins die transzendentale Konstitution alles Positiven ermöglicht . . . ," etc. The letter is printed in an appendix to Husserl's *Phänomenologische Psychologie* (The Hague, 1962), pp. 600 ff.

[18] *Kritik der reinen Vernunft,* A 154, B 193.

[19] Like Kant, Heidegger wants something more from the word *überhaupt* than the ordinary German sense of "in general," with its unwelcome implication of "on the average." Where the word translates into English at all, one might best read: "at an ontological/transcendental level."

[20] The relationship is the subject of Husserl's *Formale und transzendentale Logik,* published in the *Jahrbuch für Philosophie und phänomenologische Forschung* in 1929, a few months before the first edition of *Vom Wesen des Grundes.*

[21] To avoid a neologism, we have written "surpassing" for both the common noun, *Überstieg,* and the less frequent gerund, *Übersteigen.* Both derive from the verb *übersteigen,* which in ordinary German, and a few times in the above passage, means "to step over" or "cross."

[22] Heidegger cannot, of course, agree with the views expressed in the foregoing paragraph, or indeed throughout much of the following section. In German, when one has reservations about what one is saying, one normally uses the subjunctive. Heidegger, however, seldom does, and his indicatives should not lead the reader, as they often have commentators, into attributing to him the very positions that he wishes to criticize.

[23] This is the only point at which Heidegger uses, and our "constitute" translates, Husserl's term *konstituieren.* Elsewhere "constitute" and "constitution" render the verb *ausmachen* (sometimes: "make up") and the noun *Verfassung* ("makeup").

[24] Heidegger's most succinct definition of "Da-

sein" is "the basic mode of the Being of man." He di-
vides the term with a hyphen here to develop its root
meaning, "Being . . . there," which he unfolds in *Sein
und Zeit,* § 3: "Das Da-sein hat sein Da zu sein. Weil
das Wesen des Daseins darin liegt, daß es je sein Sein
als seiniges zu sein hat, ist der Titel Dasein als reiner
Seinsausdruck zur Bezeichnung dieses Seienden
(Mensch) gewählt."

[25] Husserl distinguished two epistemological
standpoints: the "natural," or "dogmatic," and the
"transcendental." The former has as its "correlate" the
"natural world," to justify our knowledge of which we
suspend the natural and thus reach the transcendental
standpoint. From here we survey "the whole field of
absolute consciousness," within which the natural
world is constituted and our knowledge of it grounded.
Cf. Husserl, *Ideen zu einer reinen Phänomenologie und
phänomenologischen Philosophie* (The Hague, 1950),
Book One, §§ 27, 50, 62.

[26] Husserl defines *Transzendenz* as the necessarily incomplete "manner of givenness" (*Gegeben-
heitsart*) of things in the natural world. Cf. his *Ideen,*
Book One, § 42: "Zum Ding als solchem. . . ." However, he often uses the term for the natural world itself,
and it is this usage that Heidegger is scrutinizing.

[27] "Region" (*Region*) is a Husserlian term,
roughly synonymous with "class" in ordinary philosophical usage; its strictly phenomenological meaning
is defined in *Ideen,* Book One, § 16.

[28] On Heidegger's definition, something is *ex-
istenzial* if it pertains to the ontological features of
Dasein, and *existenziell,* on the other hand, if it pertains
to Dasein's ontic features or affairs, i.e., to Dasein's
affairs prior to the clarification of its ontological structure. Cf. *Sein und Zeit,* § 4.

[29] *Schulmetaphysik* is a popular name for the
school of Christian Wolff (1679–1754). Its adherents,

among them Crusius and Baumgarten, sought to codify the philosophy of Leibniz in "geometrical fashion," deducing his conclusions from irrefutable axioms and definitions, then enlarging them in corollaries and scholia.

[30] *Kennen* and *erkennen,* like the French *connaître* and *savoir,* both mean "to know," *kennen* in the sense of "be acquainted with" (*connaître*) and *erkennen* in the sense of "know for certain that" (*savoir*). Their cognate nouns, *Kenntnis* and *Erkenntnis,* we have translated as "knowledge about" and "knowledge of."

[31] Cf. *Sein und Zeit,* §§ 53–58. The word "being" functions strictly as a present participle in the phrase "potentiality for being" and should not be confused with the gerund *Seiendes.*

[32] The criticisms are made of Max Scheler. Cf. his *Vom Ewigen im Menschen,* ed. Maria Scheler (4th ed.; Bern, 1954), pp. 308 ff.

[33] Heidegger asks the same question in *Sein und Zeit,* p. 64, and later on (p. 366) answers, much less ambiguously than in the present volume: "Wenn das 'Subjekt' ontologisch als existierendes Dasein begriffen wird, dessen Sein in der Zeitlichkeit gründet, dann muß gesagt werden: Welt ist 'subjektiv.' Diese 'subjektive' Welt aber ist dann als zeitlich-transzendente 'objektiver' als jedes mögliche 'Objekt.' "

[34] The verb *bilden* can mean "to form" in a number of senses: "to fashion" or "create," "to be" or "compose," and, intransitively, with the reflexive *sich,* "to arise" or "develop." Heidegger gives no clue as to which sense should prevail here. The noun *Bild* means: "picture," "image," "likeness," "representation," and only seldom "form." *Vorbild* normally means "pattern" or "model," but Heidegger has inserted a hyphen to bring alive its root meaning of "pre/proto-picture." Cf. Heidegger's excursus on the terms in "Die Zeit des Weltbildes," in *Holzwege,* pp. 82 ff.

[35] In everyday usage, and in the last paragraph of the present volume, the verb *zeitigen* means "to mature" or "give rise to." Yet in Heidegger it generally stands for something like "make temporal through incorporation into the projects of Dasein." Cf. *Unterwegs zur Sprache*, p. 213: "Zeitigen heißt. . . ."

[36] Kierkegaard used the term "secret" as a metaphor for the "pure inwardness" of the believer's relationship to the Eternal or "Transcendent." The nature of the relationship is like a secret in the sense that it cannot be told, or rather, can only be compromised in the telling. It must instead be communicated in "indirect discourse," or "maieutics," and even "maieutics" is inadequate, Kierkegaard writes in his *Journals*, since it can merely teach us when the relationship is improper. For "indirect communication" cf. his *Training in Christianity* (London, 1941), pp. 132–43.

[37] The phrase is one that Socrates uses in the *Theaetetus*, 189–90, while explaining what he means by "conceiving." When Heidegger writes that "the tendency to construe the Ideas as innate in the subject" was prefigured in Plato, he is doubtless referring to Socrates' digression on the matter a few pages later (192 ff.).

[38] *Vernunft* means "reason" in the sense of a faculty or mental process or ideal, a sense that the term never shares with *Grund*. It derives from the verb *vernehmen*, "to perceive," which it follows here. Heidegger seldom uses the term himself; his quotation marks indicate that Kant's notion of "reason" is under examination.

[39] Certain critics, in reviewing *Sein und Zeit*, suggested that Heidegger was following Karl Barth and Emil Brunner in giving the same weight to the "transcendence of Being" that the two theologians gave to the "transcendence of revelation."

[40] As mentioned above, Husserl often cautioned

Heidegger against working from an "anthropological" or "anthropocentric" standpoint, a standpoint that is "still dogmatic" in that it has not been clarified in the transcendental reduction. For an elaboration of his cautionings cf. his 1931 Berlin lecture, published as "Philosophy and Anthropology" in R. Chisholm (ed.), *Realism and the Background of Phenomenology* (Glencoe, 1960).

[41] Though Husserl never, to our knowledge, uses the term *Standpunktsfreiheit,* he sometimes mentions that the transcendental reduction (epochē) frees the pure ego from any particular point of view and leaves the field of consciousness "anonymous," making a scientific inquiry about its contents possible. Cf., for example, *Die Krisis der europäischen Wissenschaften und die transzendentale Phänomenologie,* ed. W. Biemel (The Hague, 1962), p. 188: ". . . die ganze Scheidung und Ordnung der Personalpronomina ist in meiner Epoche zum Phänomen geworden, mitsamt dem Vorzug des Ich-Mensch unter anderen Menschen. . . ."

[42] *Umwillen* ("for the sake of . . .") is a preposition that Heidegger often uses as a technical noun. It is discussed in *Sein und Zeit,* §§ 18, 41. The component *willen* corresponds to "sake" in the English and, as in English, cannot be used outside a prepositional phrase, e.g., *um Gottes willen* ("for God's sake") or *meinerwillen* ("for my sake"). Heidegger, in the following sentences, puns on its etymological kinship with *Wille,* or "will." We might, then, paraphrase the passage as follows: if "world" is understood as the totality of what exists "for the sake of" Dasein, i.e., for its own peculiar uses, then Dasein's "sake" (*Wille*) can be said to create, or fashion, the uses in terms of which it deals with the world.

[43] Throughout the following passage, Heidegger juxtaposes different verbs with the component *werfen* ("throw"): *entwerfen* ("project" or "throw off"), *überwerfen* ("throw over"), and *vorwerfen* ("reproach" or

"throw forth/to"). *Entwurf,* the cognate noun of *entwerfen,* follows closely the sense and etymology of the English "project." Yet in ordinary German it can, and in Heidegger often does, mean either "sketch" or "outline," or—in the sense that a statistician or geometer, but not a psychologist, might use the word—"projection."

[44] Heidegger makes a transitive verb of *Welt* ("world"), as he did earlier with *Nichts* ("nothing"), evidently to encourage the reader to think of *Welt* and *Nichts* as existing, or functioning, in a way so peculiarly their own that it can only be expressed tautologically.

[45] The criterion is Kant's. Cf. his *Kritik der reinen Vernunft,* A 533, B 561, where freedom is defined as "das Vermögen, einen Zustand *von selbst* anzufangen, dessen Kausalität also nicht nach dem Naturgesetze wiederum unter einer anderen Ursache steht, welche sie der Zeit nach bestimmte." Also A 445, B 473: "Die Freiheit . . . als eine besondere Art von Kausalität."

[46] *Stiften* means "to found" or "establish" in the sense that one establishes, not a fact, but an institution.

[47] *Boden nehmen* is a rare variation of *Boden fassen. Boden* normally means "floor" or "earth," though it has many of the same connotations as *Grund,* as in the phrases *auf dem Boden der Erfahrung* ("on the basis of experience") or *zurück auf den rauhen Boden* ("back to rough ground").

[48] *Eingenommen (von)* shares with *gestimmt (für)* the implication of "inclined in favor of" or "infatuated with."

[49] *Entgegenbringen* can also mean "to offer," so that the sentence might instead read: ". . . it offers the 'actually' realizable possibilities of the project of world *to* Dasein as its world."

[50] The reference is to Husserl. Like the earlier discussion of intentionality, the following pages seem to fulfill a promise made in a footnote in *Sein und Zeit,* p. 363, which reads: "Daß und wie die Intentionalität

des 'Bewußtseins' in der ekstatischen Zeitlichkeit *gründet* [the word is italicized only in recent editions], wird der folgende Abschnitt zeigen." One must assume, not unfairly, that *Vom Wesen des Grundes* originally formed part of the never published Third Division ("Zeit und Sein") of *Sein und Zeit*, Part One.

[51] The word in parentheses, "truth," refers to the whole phrase, "kind of disclosure" (*Enthüllungsart*).

[52] Cf. note 36, above.

[53] *Sorge*, or "care," is a technical term for "the Being of Dasein" that Heidegger discusses in *Sein und Zeit*, §§ 26, 41, 65. *Bestand* and *Beständigkeit* have many of the same equivalents: "continuance," "duration," "permanence," "stability," etc. Both derive from the verb *bestehen*, which means "to exist," with overtones of "continue" and "endure."

[54] For Leibniz' various statements of the principle of sufficient reason cf. his "Fifth Letter to Clark," § 125, and *Theodicée*, § 44; also the *Monadologie*, §§ 31–32, where it is associated with the principles of identity and contradiction, an association that Heidegger will shortly dispute.

[55] *Unwesen* has a loose range of meanings: "disorder," "abuse," "confusion," "nuisance," "mischief." The idiom *Unwesen treiben*, which Heidegger employs for the second time here, means "to be up to one's tricks" or "to play mischief with"; since the idiom is less colloquial in German, we have sought a compromise in "breeds confusion." The word's two components, "non" (*un*) and "essence" (*Wesen*), suggest the translation "(have) no essence" when, in the following paragraph, Heidegger enters a hyphen between them.

[56] In the second version of the *Encyclopaedia Britannica* article, the same which Heidegger edited, Husserl wrote that traditional philosophers had remained at a level of "undefined generality and emptiness" to the extent that they had failed to undertake the

transcendental reduction, the new and "radical departure" that would allow us to secure our knowledge of the natural world. Cf. his *Phänomenologische Psychologie,* pp. 256 f.

[57] "Iteration" is a term from Husserl. It is described in the first book of the *Ideen,* § 112, as an operation which permits one to distinguish fantasy and reflection from perception. If an experience can be "iterated," it can become, *ad infinitum,* the object of another experience of the same kind. We can have fantasies about fantasies, but not perceptions of perceptions, etc. Heidegger's thought seems to be that freedom—as that on the basis of which "reasons" become possible, as *der Grund des Grundes,*—does not in turn have, but it, its own reason.

[58] *Abgrund* commonly means "abyss" or "precipice," but Heidegger hyphenates its components here to bring its root meaning, "non/off-ground," into play. As the *Abgrund* of Dasein, freedom is that to which Dasein looks, and beyond which it cannot look, in search of reasons or causes.